T0195870

I'm Praying,
and I Won't Get Up:
Establishing and Solidifying Your Relationship with God Through Prayer

Rev. Dr. H. Elaine Joyner

Order this book online at www.trafford.com
or email orders@trafford.com

Most Trafford titles are also available at major online book retailers.

Print information available on the last page.

ISBN: 978-1-6987-1173-7 (sc)
ISBN: 978-1-6987-1174-4 (e)

Trafford rev. 04/21/2022

 www.trafford.com

North America & international
toll-free: 844-688-6899 (USA & Canada)
fax: 812 355 4082

CONTENTS

Dedication vii
Preface ix
Introduction xiii

Caught in the Act: Repentance in Prayer-God Forgives 1
I Want to Go to College: God Sent Me An Angel 13
Through the Storm 20
No Marriage for Me—Why, God? 26
Intercessory Prayer... 32
Write the Book.. 37
Graduate School: God Knows Best................................... 46
Keep You from Falling 52
He Woke Me Up This Morning,
and Started Me on My Way 58
"Order My Steps" 62
More Than I Could Ever Imagine… 67
God's Got You—God Gave Me More Time.................... 74
Guardian Angel.. 78
A Bad Decision: God Restored Me 83

Desires of the Heart: From Doctoral
Student to Seminary Teacher... 90
Already Worked It Out: Joiner and Joan............................ 97
Fortifying A Flattened Faith... 104
The Importance of Prayer... 121

DEDICATION

To the young in my family...

Tiffany, Steven, James, Jr., Paden, Danielle, Quita, Kamri, CJ, Davian, Taylor, Aliyah, Will, Nicholas, Quintin, Jamila, Essence, Corea, Gabby, Belle, Aaron, Coreyan, Nyla, King, Mariah, Dallas, Amia:

Of all the things I've ever given you, this is the one of which I am most proud. May this book serve as an example of how you can recognize and weave God into your everyday lives and have a relationship with God that is so solid that your journey through life is nothing less than healthy, peaceful, successful, and full of joy. God is real, ready, and waiting. Trust in that fact, and trust in him. I love you forever.

PREFACE

In this age in which "cool churches" and seed-sowing for the purpose of financial gain are common and contagious realities, a book on prayer might seem a bit antiquated or irrelevant to the unchurched (and maybe even to the [misguided] Christian). Unfortunately, we live in a time in which our happiness depends upon our material possessions—the size of them, the amount of them, and the labels that are displayed upon them ((authentic or fake). We long for things we cannot afford and things for which we have not worked. We long for people, with whom we are compatible (or not), and upon whom we can place the burden of our own happiness or completeness. This present age of the "cool church" and the prosperity gospel is a most-perfect age for the *bold* assertion of prayer, with an even bolder assertion/demand for a response from God. There is need in this society to return to that which we can do to effect change in our lives. *God, I'm Praying, and I Won't Get Up: Establishing and Solidifying a Relationship with God Through Prayer* purports to re-designate prayer as the default mechanism for the attainment of peace, promise, and positivity in our everyday lives in conjunction with the development of a personal relationship with God.

This book originates from two sermons preached by my former pastor, Reverend Dr. Charles B. Jackson, Sr., of the Brookland Baptist Church in West Columbia, South Carolina. The first sermon, entitled, "Without God, We Cannot and Without Us, God Will Not," suggests that without God, humans can do nothing, and without humans, God will do nothing. In other words, as we need God for things to happen in our lives, so does God require our agency for things to happen in our lives. In retrospective examination of my faith life, I realize that while his sermonic message deals primarily with human agency and God's response, it simultaneously promotes relationship with God— relationship that, through the interaction between humans and God, nurtures an elevated level of faith and trust, and consequently builds a confidence that emboldens humans to expect/demand a response from God, which results in a solidified relationship between humans and God.

The second sermon emphasized the imperative of prayer. In it, Pastor Jackson not only taught us the importance of prayer, but he also taught us how to pray, asserting, "When you pray, don't just pray and get up; stay down there, and wait for God to answer, for God will answer you." Being a novice in my faith at the time, I found this word compelling. I knew that I was going to do as instructed. I did not do it immediately, however, but one day I found myself in a desperate situation in which I needed support and guidance from God and God alone. At that moment, I remembered the pastor's instructions; I followed them, and God answered. I tried it again, and God answered. From then on, I made it a model of my prayer to pray, stay down, and wait on God's response. What I realized was that not only were my prayers being answered (favorably or not), I found myself developing a life-changing relationship with God that would last throughout my years. It is this relationship that I have developed through prayer that has brought me joy throughout my life, peace throughout my life, and achievement throughout my life, and that I want to share with the rest of the world in order that you may receive and achieve the same.

INTRODUCTION

Do you want to be so close to God that God answers your prayers immediately, and so loudly and clearly that you know without a doubt that it's God? Are you tired of trying to make sense of your life and feeling disconnected from God while others around you appear as though they and God are best friends? Do you long for your own special relationship with God and often ask yourself, "How can I get to know God like that"? If so, then this book is for you.

God, I'm Praying, and I Won't Get Up: Establishing and Solidifying Your Relationship with God Through Prayer is a book that asserts the power of prayer in not only evoking a response from God, but also in the development of a strong relationship with God. The author suggests the notion that when you faithfully go to God in prayer, God will answer you for your good. This book comprehensively demonstrates not only the power of prayer, but also the comforting intimacy of God's omnipresence and the possibility of relationship-building with God through prayer. God reveals Godself to us most clearly as God responds to our prayers: and this revelatory clarity results in the solidification of an intimate relationship with God—one in which the pray-er can recognize the response as both God-sent and intended for one's good. It is also my belief that the trajectory toward an intimate relationship with God cyclically intertwines need, desire, belief, faith, prayer, and God's response. Hebrews 11:6 says, "But without faith, it is impossible to please him; for he that cometh to God must believe that he (God) is, and that he (God) is a rewarder of them that diligently seek him." It is our faith that pleases God. God rewards our faith by giving us our needs and the desires of our hearts. In return, our faith continues to grow, we hasten to God more, we trust God more, and rely more deeply upon God. Consequently, because of the faithfulness that God repeatedly has shown, as we encounter life's trials or find ourselves in need, instead of panicking and being thrown into despair, we simply rely on our solid relationship with God, and hasten to God's throne. Ultimately, what results is the establishment and solidification of our relationship with God.

The structural makeup of authentic experience, scriptural support, supplicatory prayer, God's answer, lesson learned, and song is strung through each account in this book. Developing a relationship with God encompasses the employment of all these elements. It is my passionate desire for everyone to have a solid relationship with God. It is only through such a relationship that one can have joy and peace through every waking moment, and through every trial and tribulation. This is not something that I knew at the time these experiences occurred, however. Developing a relationship that's solid takes time and work; hence, it is a journey. *God, I'm Praying, and I Won't Get Up: Establishing and Solidifying a Relationship with God Through Prayer* aims to steer you on your journey trajectory towards intimacy with God. In this book you will find first-hand accounts of evidenced communication between human and deity, which purports to demonstrate the omnipresence of God and the intimacy, faith, and trust that can be obtained through a prayer relationship with God. It exemplifies relationship development and solidification through a series of human experiences, and thus, aims to guide you in dealing with your life's situations by following the same model: fervent prayer and supplication, the application of scripture, and the demonstration of God's faithfulness through God's resolve. It is a book of experiences— true glimpses of ways in which God has been faithful to me, provided for me, shielded me, assured me, humbled me, forgiven me, and more; prayerfully, you will conceive the notion that if God did those things for me, then God can and will do the same and more for you.

Alongside the experiential accounts, you will find scriptures that serve as the backdrops of my faith and scriptural validation of these occurrences. As a lover of song, I have also included some compatible songs, as well. These three components (experience, scripture, and song) are the undergirds of my faith life and the development of my relationship with God.

I pondered the notion of relationship—how can one expect or demand an answer to one's prayer immediately from God without ever having had some prior relationship with God that has already been built. I can assert that this relationship is based on mutual effort by both humans and God: faith and prayer by humans and continual blessings by God. This relationship revolves in a circular motion, moving from faith to prayer and supplication, and then receiving blessings from God in response. Of course, all blessings are not responses to our prayers. In fact, most of them are simply gracious gifts from God, demonstrations of God's grace and mercy. Yet, I assert from my own experiences, that God indeed will bless you in response to your prayers, and, because you have experienced God's responsiveness, you will know upon receipt of the blessing, that it came from nobody but God. Thus, an increase in your faith and trust, and an increase in the development of your relationship with God, and the delightful inclination to go to God (hasten) again in prayer to start the cycle again. It is this cyclic faithful and trusting relationship that has sustained me throughout my life. Let it do the same for you.

This book is real. The stories are real, and thus, are reflective of my imperfections. We all know that in our humanity, there are mistakes, bad decisions, and to put it simply, wrongdoings. The reader may not agree with the things or the circumstances or the situations about which you read; they stem solely from my humanness and my own firsthand experiences. It is only through these lenses that I can share with you because these are my experiences. I petition you to abandon the judgment. And take this book at face value. God did. God showed Godself to me despite my flaws, despite my bad decisions, despite my mistakes. This speaks volumes to the purpose God had placed upon my life at birth. Having gone through the things that I've gone through and made the decisions I have made, God still saw fit to show God's faithfulness to me, so that I can share my experiences of who God is with all of you and, just maybe, help you along the way. I pray that this book is a blessing to you all.

Caught in the Act: Repentance in Prayer-God Forgives

Scriptures:

"You will never succeed in life if you try to hide your sins. Confess them and give them up; then God will show mercy to you." Proverbs 28:13 (ESV)

"Repent, then, and turn to God, so that He will forgive your sins." Acts 3:19 (GNT)

"...if my people who are called by my name will humble themselves, and pray and seek My face, and turn from their wicked ways, then I will hear from heaven, and will forgive their sin and heal their land." 2 Chronicles 7:14 (NKJV)

I grew up hearing in church that God is a forgiving God, and that all we have to do is pray and repent and God would forgive us. I distinctly remember the preacher saying that "it doesn't matter what you have done; God will forgive you. Just go to God in prayer, tell God you're sorry, and God will forgive you." I remember wondering as a child if that were really true, and if this God would do that for me.

I was a cheerleader in the twelfth grade at my high school. We got a new cheerleader from another school. She was kind of cool. We began to hang out and some of us walked home from school one day. There was a group of us. We stopped by Kmart to get some popcorn, and I remember them saying that they were going to steal some things. I asked how they were going to do that, and they told me to just watch. So, we entered the store and walked over to the clothing section. They picked clothes they liked and stuck the items into the clothing rack, along with their purses. We walked to the front door. And they yelled, "Run!" And we took off running out of the store. I was amazed! Afraid, but amazed. We ran through the parking lot and across the street, laughing all the way.

At Christmas time I didn't have much money. But I wanted to get everyone in the family a Christmas gift. I remembered what we had done that day at Kmart, so I had the bright idea that I was going to go to try that same theft technique by myself. I did not want anyone to know that I would do such a thing. I went to the store, picked out some gifts for my family, and placed them in my buggy. Then I did as we had done before— I walked to the clothing rack, slid my over-sized burgundy floral suede purse between the clothes on the rack, and dropped the items from the cart into my purse. And before I could finish putting all the items in my purse, I heard a voice telling me to stop what I was doing, put my hands by my side, and follow them. I looked up and found that there were gentlemen standing all around me. Oh my God! I had been caught stealing.

I cannot tell you the feelings that came over me. I was so embarrassed. I didn't want anybody to know, but I could not hide. I was a cheerleader at my school and an "A" and "B" student, and I was wearing my cheerleader jacket. If everybody found out that I went to jail, I would never hear the end of it. I could never face them again. And oh, how afraid I was at my mother finding out that I had done something so reckless! My mother was a corporal punishment enforcer. She was a beast with her whooping! I did not want her to find out. I was scared to pieces.

Security led me to a small room. They read me my rights and told me I could make one phone call. There was no way I was going to call my mother; I opted to call my biological father instead. I told him what happened, and he spoke to one of the officers, who told him they were taking me downtown to the city jail. "Me, jail? Oh, my God, No!"

The walk from the back of the store to the police car was horrendous! Everybody was standing around looking. I felt as though I was in a humiliation parade. I tried to hide by putting my head down, but I couldn't hide; I had that jacket on. The ride in the police car was horrific. I laid down in the backseat so that no one could see me. The officer asked me why I had done it and I told him in tears that I just wanted to get Christmas gifts for my family. He told me that he was sorry that I was in trouble and that only made me cry more. I was fingerprinted at the jail and placed into a cell with two other females. As I entered the cell, I heard them whispering. Then I heard one of them say, "Uh-huh, and she's cute, too." I was terrified! I cried and I cried and cried some more, for what seemed like hours.

Suddenly, a guard came to the cell door. He had someone with him. My Uncle Bobby, who then was one of the deputy sheriffs with the County Sheriff's Office, came into the cell. Boy, was I glad to see him! I hugged him so tightly. I cried and I cried and cried. He just let me cry. He said, "Black Beauty, what are you doing in here?" I told him that I was trying to get everybody a Christmas present. His reply was, "Black Beauty, you have messed up your whole life!" All I could say was, "I'm sorry! I'm sorry! I'm sorry!" I couldn't stop crying. I couldn't stop crying! So, he told me to stop crying. "Black Beauty, stop crying. It's gonna be okay." He waited until I stopped. I asked him if I could go home with him, to please take me home with him. I did not want him to leave me there.

My uncle told me that I could not go home that night, but my mom and stepdad would be in to get me in the morning; then I could go home. Well, that was all I needed to hear— Mama knew about this. And she would be picking me up in the morning. Oh, Lawd, did I know what I was in for, even at seventeen years old! I was in big trouble. And I deserved it. I didn't know which one to fear more – the coming night or my mom the next morning. That was all I could think about all night. I cried myself to sleep.

The next morning, I could not wait to get out. They came and got me at about 8:30. I walked out so frighteningly because I knew I was in trouble with my mom. However, when I saw her and my dad, I could not be happier. I ran and hugged her. We stood before the judge. He said some things I did not understand, but later I learned that I was released on my own personal recognizance. Whew! I was glad that was over! We walked to the car very quietly.

When I got into the backseat and we got to rolling, I spoke first. I knew I was in trouble, and I knew I was going to get it; so, I spoke first. "Mama, I'm sorry." However, instead of Mom fussing as I had anticipated, my stepdad interrupted: "Elaine, how could you do such a thing? I mean, what were you thinking?" My daddy never fussed at me, so to hear him yelling at me was painful, in itself. And I knew if he was that mad, how much angrier Mom was at me.

But much to my surprise what happened next could only have been an act of God. Instead of yelling at me, instead of threatening to half-kill me, instead of talking angrily to me, what my mom said has remained with me all the days of my life and will continue to remain with me as an example of God's love for me. My mom interrupted my dad in the middle of his rant, "All right, Thomas, leave her alone. She has been through enough." If I tell you that my mom's compassion whooped me more than any physical whipping ever could, you can believe it. I loved her so much more for it. Mommy's love for me showed me the compassion of God, the compassion of a mother, and the true forgiveness of God. And not to mention, it was on that day that I learned that my mom was indeed human, if you know what I mean. I had disappointed her. I had hurt her. And I felt awful about it. Yet, she had shown her goodness to me. She had shown her love to me; now it is my turn to show good. I didn't know what to do, however.

All I knew was what I had heard my Pastor say at church (that God is a forgiving God). I knew at that moment that I needed God to forgive me right now. I needed forgiveness like I had never needed it before. I needed God's love to assure me that I was good, too. I needed God's love to assure me that I was not bad. So, I just cried in the backseat of the car. I cried tears of regret, I cried tears of sorrow and sadness that I had disappointed my mom and dad, and I cried tears of gratitude for God's mercy on me regarding my mother's punishment. We said not another word in the car. Just my tears, just my sniffles, just my guilt.

When we got into the house, I went straight to my room. I took off the jacket, for I didn't want to ever wear it again. I had brought shame to the cheerleaders at the school. I had brought shame to myself, shame to my mom and dad, and shame to my biological daddy. I had brought shame to my uncle and my family. So, I went straight to my room. I told myself that I was going to do what the Pastor taught us to do whenever we found ourselves in trouble after having done wrong. I was going to lie stretched out on the floor, and give it all to God—hiding nothing, or holding back nothing. I realized that this was not a time for embarrassment, pride, haughtiness, or arrogance. This was a time for humility.

I never expected that I would need God to be forgiving of me for something like this. I needed God to hear my prayer because I needed God's love. I knew I had to hold on to God's love. And it was at this moment that my relationship with God was absolutely solidified; I had experienced its existence. And I also realized that for the rest of my life I could never judge another person because I had my own wrongs. I had my own weaknesses. I had my own skeletons. I was nobody to judge another person. And I felt at that moment that I never would. I got down on the floor I stretched out and began to pray.

Prayer:

"Dear God, I lie here in tears. I'm so ashamed. Please forgive me. Please forgive me. I messed up so big. I did something so stupid. I did something careless. I did something irresponsible. I broke the law. Oh, God help me. Help me. Mama didn't teach me to do that. I was trying to get Christmas gifts for everybody, but I know I went about it the wrong way. God, please forgive me. I have let everybody down, Lord." The tears wouldn't stop falling. "God, please, please forgive me. Please, oh God, please forgive me. I will never do it again! I will never, ever do it again! I promise! I'm sorry for shoplifting. I'm sorry for stealing. Forgive me, oh God. God don't ever leave me, please. I need you forever. I love you forever. Reverend Fair said that you are a forgiving God. I need you to forgive me, please…Please…Please… In the name of Jesus Christ, our Lord, I pray. Amen."

I did not get up. I could not get up. I needed God to know that at that very point in my life, I was putting to use what I had heard and learned in church. I needed God to hear me. I needed God to know that I was for real in what I was saying, that my tears were for real, and that I was desperate. It was at that point that not only was I calling on God, but I was also surrendering to a life with God for the rest of my life. I mean, how could I prove to God my promise of never doing that again if I didn't have God close to me always?

Simply put, this moment of prayer and repentance, faith, and trust, was the beginning of my true walk with God— never to leave God in the future, consulting God always, fearing God in wisdom, believing in God's ever-presence and

God's forgiveness. And most of all believing in God's love for me. No, I did not get up. In fact, I fell asleep there on the floor. I awoke, glad to know that that ordeal was over.

It Ain't Over

A few weeks later, my mom told me that I could not go to school the next day because we had to go to court about the incident. "What," I thought to myself. "The incident? I thought that was over when you all drove me out of there, when I prayed to God and God forgave me, when God showed me forgiveness through Mom. There's more? What? Why? Why, God? Are you not going to let me forget this ever?" All of these were my inner thoughts.

The next morning, Mama, Daddy, and I drove to a nearby branch of the County Judicial System. "Mama, why are we going here?" I asked. "You have to see the Judge, Elaine," she replied. The Judge decides if you have to spend time in jail.

"Huh? Jail? I had been to jail already. Oh, Lord. Now, see, I took Civics in school, and made an "A." But I didn't get ANY OF THIS! What in the world?! I can't go to jail! No, not again." I became so nervous. I began to cry, and I began to pray.

Prayer:

"God, I trust you. I believe in you! I believe them at church when they say that you are a 'lawyer for the lawyer-less.' Lord, I need you now. Be a lawyer for me, please. Please don't send me to jail. Please, God, please. Help me! Amen."

Tears were streaming down my face, with Mama waiting on me by the door, I slowly got out the car. I turtle-walked my way inside, praying that I didn't see anybody I knew. I was holding to God's lawyering hand, afraid of the unknown. We entered the courthouse and then the courtroom. It was eerie. Mama, Daddy, and I just sat down quietly and waited. After about fifteen minutes, the door opened to the Judge's Chamber. "All rise," I heard someone say. What I saw next astounded me. The Judge entered, as expected, but behind him was my Uncle Bobby, speaking with the Judge. I heard him say, "She didn't mean any harm, Judge." All I could think was, "My uncle has come to help me! Lord, I hope he can help!"

"Harriet Joyner!" I heard my name called loudly. I walked down to the bench. My uncle stood with me. The Judge asked me what happened. He said, "Harriet, were you caught shoplifting in Kmart?" I responded, "Yes, Sir." He continued with another question, "Why were you shoplifting, Harriet?" I was terrified. I began to cry, but through my tears and my fears, I answered him, "I wanted to get my family some Christmas presents. I'm sorry! I am so sorry!"

The Judge began to explain that if I did not have the money, then I should not have tried to give the gifts. He explained that my family would have loved me anyway, which I knew they would have done. It was very nice of him to say that. However, he then turned into disciplinary mode.

"Harriet," he began. "What you did was wrong. While I know you were trying to get gifts for your family, stealing is not acceptable under any circumstance. I know that your family would not want you giving gifts to them that you have stolen from the local store. I am going to let you go this time, Harriet. I'm going to place this case in my desk. And I'm going to keep it there. However, if you ever come back to this court room again, I am going to lock you up for a long time. I won't ask any questions. I'm just going to send you to jail. Do you understand me," he asked. "Yes, Sir," I replied. "Thank you, Your Honor." My uncle and I turned and walked out of the courtroom with Mom and Dad. When we got into the car, I asked my mom, "Mama, is it over?" "Yes, Elaine, it's over." More tears... "Thank you, God!"

Lesson:

According to belief.net, the need to repent of your sins is a central belief in Christianity. Accepting Jesus Christ into your life and asking Him to cleanse you of your sins is the only true way to live an eternal life in heaven. True repentance leads a person to say "I have sinned" in an honest, regretful acknowledgement of the sin with a commitment to change.

God is everything we need. God is a lawyer, a doctor, a friend. God is right there when we need God to be. We are not perfect. We are human, and in our humanity, we make mistakes. God is right there to forgive us if we repent and turn away from those mistakes, never to offend in that way again. We need to be aware of the many facets of God.

As we continue to pray and discover the various aspects of God, we are developing our relationship with God. We are developing a relationship with God in which we recognize God's presence and God's power and embrace the fact that God will share both of these things with us when we are in need. And as we recognize God's omnipresence and omnipotence, we realize that it is God to whom we should turn when we find ourselves in our difficult situations. We should not turn to anyone else other than God when we find ourselves in need. Thus, the relationship becomes one of human's trust and faith in God and God's faithfulness to humans as believers. The more we see God's faithfulness to us, the more we should be inclined to go to God as a first resort, rather than a last resort, solidifying even greater our relationship with God.

The last lesson from this experience is that God will forgive. I am living proof of that. Sometimes, however, we have to learn to forgive ourselves. God has already forgiven us, and ofttimes we will still be condemning ourselves for the wrong that we have done because we cannot forgive ourselves. I cried so much about this ordeal. I cry even as I write this. I had to realize, however, that if God, to whom we are accountable, yet whom we disappoint, can forgive us, then we must be able to forgive ourselves and others. Knowing that we have been forgiven by God gives us confidence, for we are not hopeless, but rather, we are loved. Rushing to God's throne is an imperative in the process of establishing and solidifying our relationship with God. We must learn to hasten to God's throne.

Rev. Dr. H. Elaine Joyner

Song:

Surely God is Able

Surely, surely, surely, surely,
God is able to carry you through.
He's a doctor for the doctor-less
He's a lawyer for the lawyer-less
He's a mother for the motherless,
He's a father for the fatherless,
Surely, surely, surely, surely,
God is able to carry you through.

I Want to Go to College: God Sent Me An Angel

Scriptures:

"For he will command his angels concerning you to guard you in all your ways."

Psalm 91:11 ESV

"For it is written, "'He will command his angels concerning you, to guard you."

Luke 4:10 (ESV)

I was an ambitious young southern and country lady back in the day. I thought I could do it all. I tried my hand at gardening, but I have to say that a horticulturalist I was not. Yes, I planted my garden, with fruits and vegetables in it; and yes, they did grow, and I was proud. I planted cucumbers, okra, tomatoes, squash, green beans, peppers, and the like. We ate them for lunch, dinner, snacks, and everything in between. I was so proud. I have to be honest, however, and tell you that they all were small in size. I could not get them to grow big. However, my best friend's father in the house over the fence behind our house grew the biggest vegetables I'd ever seen. And our next-door neighbor, my mother's best friend's husband, Mr. Thomas, grew amazingly large crops, as well. So, I would ask Mr. Thomas to please tell me how he did it. And now that I reflect on it, he never told me what he did to make those things so big. I know my girlfriend's father used minnows. He used to throw those little fish all over his garden. I didn't know where to get minnows, so I couldn't try that. I do remember Mr. Thomas telling me he used cow manure. So I purchased some cow manure and applied it to my garden; it didn't help. So, it wasn't intended for me to be a serious gardener as they were. I just didn't have a green thumb.

I did my gardening through high school and beyond. When I wasn't gardening, I was trying to make the yard as pretty as the neighbors' yards by raking leaves and such. Upon graduation from high school, I did not go straight to college. I owed my high school some fees, so, until I paid them, I could not get my transcripts to in order to apply for college.

I got my first job at McDonald's soon after graduating from high school. While working there I encountered or many of my white classmates who had also graduated, but were planning to attend college in the fall. This was where I heard them talk about many things about which I did not know and was not even familiar. They talked about going to college and their college experiences. They talked about having their own checking accounts (opened and supported by their parents). I remember thinking to myself, "Gee, I want my own checking account." As they began attending college and working, and I continued working there only, they would come back on the weekends and talk about their experiences. I thought to myself thinking to myself,

"Gee, I want to go to college. Why can't I go to college like my classmates?" So, I uttered a prayer to God.

Prayer:

"God, I want to go to college, too."

My heart was heavy, because by then I had realized I could not live off the money I was making. I realized that a McDonald's salary would not be sufficient for a quality livelihood, for which I longed. I really wanted to go to college. I owed my high school $225. With the checks that I was making from McDonald's I did not know when I would be able to save that much money to go get my transcripts. I dismissed the idea of going to college and just continued working at McDonald's.

One afternoon while I was raking the yard, Mr. Thomas called me over to the fence, as he did often when we chatted about the garden. He began talking to me and asking me about college. "Harriet, why aren't you in college?" I replied, "Well, I want to go, but I still owe my school some money for fees, and I can't get my transcripts to apply until I pay them." He then asked how much I owed the school. I told him that I owed $225, and that Mama and Daddy didn't have it to pay; in fact, they said they were finished paying for me. Mr. Thomas replied, "Harriet, you need to be in college." I told him that I agreed with him. I wanted nothing more than to be able to have my own checking account, and get an education so that I could make more money. So, I walked away from him saying that he was correct and that I really wanted to go. I went on into the house for the evening.

God's Answer:

The next time I was in the yard, Mr. Thomas came to the out and called me over to the fence. I met him over there and he asked me, "Harriet, if you had the money to pay your fees, would you go enroll yourself in college?" And I said "Yes sir, I would." And then, the most amazing thing happened. Mr. Thomas pulled out an envelope and handed it to me over the fence, and said, "Harriet, go get yourself in college."

Oh, my goodness! I thanked Mr. Thomas and told him I would pay him twenty-five dollars every paycheck. I ran in the house and put that money under my mattress. I was so excited to know that I was going to pay my fees and enroll in college! I went over to my school and stated that I was there to pay my fees. I was directed to the counselor, Mr. M. He pulled out my file and examined my record. He had a very puzzled look on his face and I wondered what was wrong. What he said to me saddens me to this day. "Hmmm," he said. "I don't know how we missed you. I don't know why we could've missed you." I asked him what he meant, what he was referring to, and he told me that I was in the top twenty-five percent of the class, and I should have gotten a scholarship. And he did not know how they missed me." I couldn't get bent out of shape about that because there was nothing that could be done at that point. So, what the counselor vowed to do was to help me with the college application and help me get into the University. And the rest was history.

I am in tears as I write this story. This was the beginning of the best of my life. I was determined to be successful.

I was determined to have my own checking account and have the college experience. And God afforded me those opportunities. Hallelujah! Hallelujah, Halelujah to God!

I went through college, learning all I could and enjoying myself. I worked three jobs at one point to take care of myself. I paid Mr. Thomas back, on my paydays, as promised, and when I couldn't pay, I went over to him and told him I would give it the next time. He never fussed, or yelled; he simply said, "Okay."

It wasn't until I moved to Chicago and graduated with a Master's degree that I remembered how I had gotten to that point: God had sent me an angel—Mr. Thomas D. Brown. I was thanking God for the blessings of education of which I have been afforded. And then I remembered how it got started. I felt bad because I had not told him thank you, I had not invited him to a single graduation, I had seriously forgotten that this man had given me this gift of education. It was in December when I graduated. I ran to my phone and I called him. He answered the phone and I said, "Mr. Thomas, it's Elaine. How are you doing?" He answered, "Hey, Harriet. Doing fine; how are you? I told him that I was fine and that I had just graduated with my Master's degree from UIC. I told him that I was calling him to thank him and for what he did for me. And his reply was, "Awww, Harriet, I didn't do nothing." I insisted, "Yes, you did. You help me when nobody else would. I don't know where I would be right now if you had not given me that money. Thank you so very much and I'm sorry that I did not say thank you sooner. Please forgive me." "Aww, Harriet, you're all right. It's all right." I said to him, "Thank you, again," and we hung up. A short time later, he died of cancer.

Lesson:

Whenever I hear Psalm 91:11 ESV, I am warmed to tears. It is the assurance of God's true love for me and God's true faithfulness to me. I can't help but to wonder where I would be had God not sent me this angel to watch over me, to help me and guide me. I don't know where, but I can say that I know it wouldn't be here. I know this because of the options that I had at the time. I wouldn't be here. I am honored to be able to have God's attention, to be able to have God's affection. God met me where I was, according to my need. It's humbling beyond measure. I know that if God did it for me, God will do the same for you.

Another lesson I take from this narrative is that when God has chosen you to be a recipient of God's blessing, God will put people in place in your life to get the job done. It's not because of anything that you have done; it's merely because God wants to bless you. And God wants you to know that it's God who did the blessing. In other words, God sends us angels to work on God's behalf to get the blessing done that God wants to bestow upon us. Everyone who comes into your life, and everyone who has been called to be in your life is there for a reason. When God wants to bless you, He will send a relationship that bears fruit. This could be a friend, a coworker, a significant other, an old acquaintance or a new one. God puts people into your life at strategic times, because in God's omniscience, God sees the bigger picture and knows what we need. Hallelujah to Jesus!

Song:

He's That Kind of Friend

If you ever need a friend that sticks
Closer than any brother,
I recommend Jesus, Jesus;
Because He's that kind of friend.
He will never forsake you, even though
He knows everything there is to know about you;
I recommend Jesus, Jesus;
Because He's that kind of friend.

Through the Storm

Scripture:

"Then Nebuchadnezzar the king was astonished, and rose up in haste, and spake, and said unto his counsellors, "Did not we cast three men bound into the midst of the fire?" They answered and said unto the king, 'True, O king.' He answered and said, 'Lo, I see four men loose, walking in the midst of the fire, and they have no hurt; and the form of the fourth is like the Son of God.'" Daniel 3: 24-25 KJV

A good friend of mine landed a job with the U. S. Alcohol, Tobacco, and Firearms Agency and was scheduled to train in Brunswick, Georgia. I drove down there one weekend to visit. It was a bright and sunny Friday afternoon, about 4:00. I was proud of my friend and was excited to go and show my support. So, I began my journey down I-95. I was just driving and listening to music—singing and jammin' when I noticed in the distance that it looked a bit dark. I also noticed that cars had pulled over and were continuing to pull over. I had concluded that it must be raining up ahead, but I wasn't fazed by it. So in all my youthful fearlessness, I continued driving. As I drew closer, I learned that it was indeed raining, and the further I drove, the heavier it rained, and the louder and scarier the pounding of the fierce raindrops upon the hood, roof, and trunk of my new Ford Escort became. I thought to myself that I now understood why the cars had pulled over; in fact, at that moment, I realized that I should probably follow suit. I contemplated doing so, but there was no room on the sides of the road. So, I kept driving. I had to. But the farther I went, the harder the rain fell, and the faster my fearlessness diminished. I grew increasingly uneasy.

Suddenly, it became so dark that I could no longer see ahead of me. Although it was only about 5:30 in the afternoon, an hour which normally still bore high sunshine, it was now pitch- black outside, with darkness so thick and eerie that it had the feel of the midnight hour on a Halloween night. There was darkness so thick that it decreased my visibility to zero, for I could see no farther than my car's windshield. Now, I was afraid. I began to cry. And I began to cry out—

Prayer:

"God, I'm scared," I cried, holding to the steering wheel with both hands and tears streaming down my face. I wept. "Help me, I'm scared!" I knew I was in danger. I had nowhere to go. I didn't know what to do. I couldn't pull over because there was no room. I couldn't just stop in the middle of the highway, because the zero visibility would have netted someone hitting me from behind. "Help me, God! Help me, God!"

God's Answer:

The next thing I knew, I saw a person (who I believe was Jesus) standing between my windshield and the darkness. Although I found his presence amazing, I did not have time to relish in that amazement. He was motioning to me with both hands, and speaking to me with his lips, "Come on… Come on," he said. With my eyes fixated on him, tears still streaming down my face, and both hands on the wheel, I drove slowly and answered, "I'm coming! I'm coming! I'm holding on!" In a finger-snapping instant, the rain stopped, the figure flew up, and the sun shone as if it had never rained at all. I looked around in wide-eyed amazement. I looked right. I looked left. And all I could say was… "Wow!" I turned my music back up and drove on my way. The storm was over. God had literally brought me through a storm.

Lesson:

This is one of my favorite experiences to share because in it I find so many assurances. This account illustrates the notion that as God is an omnipotent God, with all power in God's hands, God is also an omnipresent God who is present and in tune with each and every one of us at our immediate times of need. That is reassuring. Not only is God in tune with us individually, but God will have and show compassion for us by stepping in at our immediate points of need. I mean, there I was, a lone young lady on a highway shared with thousands of people. A storm arose and I felt fear. Immediately I hastened to God's throne. Immediately, I called upon the Lord. I cried out to the

Lord with my voice and God heard me. God heard ME. And not only did God hear me, but God also rescued me by dispatching a figure in the image of whom I thought to be Jesus, the Son of God. I get full just remembering! Hallelujah!

In trying to examine this event objectively, I must say that when I read the scripture that I identified as relevant, I immediately related to the amazement of King Nebuchadnezzar as he saw the fourth figure in the fiery furnace. In addition, I was stricken by the final sentence in Daniel 3: 25 ESV, when the King indicated that the fourth person that he saw was like the Son of God. I related to this scripture literally, for I believed that the figure that I had seen was Jesus, the Son of God. I know that this was Old Testament text, and that Jesus was not yet among the people. In fact, Mercer's Commentary asserts that the figure in the passage was an angel. I get that. I will even accept that it was one of God's angels. However, nothing is impossible with God. Nothing is too hard for God.

I spoke about this experience with Rev. Clyde White, one of the highly-respected associate pastors of Trinity United Church of Christ, and he informed that the helper was an angel of God—that God had dispatched one of God's angels down to rescue me. This really warmed my heart. To know that God would take the time to send an angel down to me in my desperate point of need gave me an immeasurable sense of connection to God. It gave me a sense of intimacy with God, for God was close enough to me to hear my cry and send me relief. God was close enough to empathize with me and feel my fear, and comfort me by guiding me through a storm to safety. Pastor White assured me that this presence of an angel was an indication that I was special to God. I carry that assurance in my heart today. However, I want you to know that this assurance is not exclusive to me. There's nothing special about me. God hears you and your prayers, as well. God will answer you, too. All that is needed is the knowledge of and belief in God (faith), the demonstration of that faith via the supplication of your need through prayer (silent or otherwise), and the expectation of an answer. I had a need; I called out to the God who I knew had all power and who was the only one who could help me, and I received an answer. No, I did not know what the answer was going to be. Instead, I knew that God was a faithful God who had answered me before, and God would not fail me this time. Neither will God fail you.

Final Prayer:

God, you're an awesome God who sits high and looks low. You know everything about us. You who are omnipotent, have the power to be ever-present with every single one of us. You hear our cries from afar off. And you answer, O God. We are not worthy of such attention, but you deem us worthy and for that we praise you. You are awesome, you are mighty. Thank you, God, for loving us despite us. Thank you for your protection. Thank you for thinking enough of us to dispatch your angels to cover us. Thank you for hearing our cries. Keep us, God. Keep us ever-so-close., We want to establish a relationship with you—but not just any kind of relationship. Please grant us an intimate relationship. In the name of Jesus, we pray... Amen

Song:

"I Love the Lord" (Whitney Houston)

I love the Lord
He heard my cry
And pitied every groan
Long as I live
And troubles rise
I'll hasten to his throne

No Marriage for Me—Why, God?

Scripture:

"For I know the plans I have for you, declares the LORD, plans for welfare and not for evil, to give you a future and a hope." Jeremiah 29:11 (ESV)

During my first year of teaching, my boyfriend and I became engaged. We had been dating for over a year and since we both had landed good jobs, we decided it was time. I decided to move back home in order to save money for our wedding. We really had not set a date, but I knew I needed at least a year or so to save for the wedding. My mom and dad were onboard with the plan. So, during my second year of teaching, I made the move back home and was so excited.

As time progressed, my boyfriend landed an even better job. It required that he relocated to a nearby state. I saw him every weekend, for either I drove to him, or he drove to me. We set a wedding date and went and picked out my ring; the engagement became more official. Well, by this time, I knew that I needed to get the ball rolling with my wedding gown.

I wanted a beautiful one and I planned to spend a pretty penny on it. Before I did, however, I consulted God. I simply uttered a prayer of guidance and approval.

Prayer:

"Okay, God," I said. I'm about to spend my money on this wedding." "Please," I continued. "If it's not right for me, please give me a sign. Amen." Then I forgot the prayer.

A little over a week or so later, I received a call at work from my fiancé. He told me how he had worked undercover the night before and had been shot at by a drug dealer. He described how he had bought drugs as an undercover agent and then when he disclosed his identity the dealer told him he did not care who he was, and that the dealer shot at him through his car window. He told how he jumped out of his vehicle and ran down the street in an effort to get to safety, but how the drug dealer had chased him. The story was so frightening. It was just so frightening. I was just glad to know that he was okay.

He then stated that he was coming back home because it had all been too much for him. He confided that he had been mentally traumatized; therefore, he thought it was best that he checked himself into a healthcare facility to get his head clear. He asked if he could leave the car at my mother's house, and of course, I agreed. He drove back to town the next day and I drove him to a healthcare facility called Charter. I was glad to know that he was about to get some help. When he had checked in completely, the officials informed me that I could come to visit him in two weeks. We said goodbye, and I left. I had a very numb feeling because I felt so sorry for him. That must have been an awful thing to have gone through. I thought about how frightened he must have been. I cried for him.

Two weeks seemed to take forever to go by. I did not speak to him. I could not call him. All the while, however, I wondered how he was. When the day finally arrived for me to visit, I went anxiously. Immediately upon seeing him, we embraced, and cried. Well, I cried. I asked how he was, and he said he was okay. He said that the first few nights were really rough on him, for he had had nightmares and cried a lot. Anyway, I was just so glad to see him.

The "Family and Friends Day" visit operated on a strategic agenda. At first there was the one-on-one greeting (which we'd had), followed by an open group meeting. The open group meeting was very enlightening. Each resident took a turn introducing him/herself, followed by a descriptor. "Hi, my name is Mary, and I am an alcoholic." "Hi, I am John, and I am addicted to prescription drugs." Or "Hi, I'm Larry and I am a coke addict." I found those introductions to be very peculiar. Questions began to race in my head. "What kind of place is this? Coke addict? Prescription drugs? Alcoholic? These folk here are in bad shape. I'm glad my man doesn't have those issues. Hmph! My man is here for only a little bit of trauma counseling. That's all. They are going to look at him like he's crazy, and probably ask, 'Is that all you are here for?' I already know it. I'm glad I'm not their family members. Matter of fact, it's my man's turn now."

My fiance' rose to his feet, gave his greeting, said his name, and looked straight at me as he confessed, "...and I am an alcoholic and cocaine addict." I tried to hold my composure. I was in utter shock! "An alcoholic and cocaine addict? For real? You told me that you were here because of the mental trauma you had undergone. For real? For real? I need some answers."

The next segment of the day was one-on-one visitation, in order that we might have our questions answered. And, boy, did I ask! He answered them. But none too sufficiently. I was still in utter disbelief. I did not understand how I could have missed something so big as this. We had lunch, said our goodbyes until the next week when the rest of his family would come. He gave me the assignment of going to get his things from his out-of-state apartment, and finalizing his affairs at his job.

When I got to his apartment, I found baking soda in the refrigerator, spoons that were burned at the bottom. Now that I had a new perspective, I realized that the spoons were not rusty because they were cheap, as I had concluded upon my first sight of them; instead, he had used them to fix his drugs. The baking soda that he kept in the refrigerator was not there as an air freshener, as I had believed in my mind, but it, too, was used for drug purposes. He also had pawned his television for cash. I began to cry. I could not believe what was happening.

The next stop was his job. I went directly to his supervisor and what I learned shocked me to no end. My fiancé lied to me about the whole incident. He was not undercover as he had stated. He had not been undercover at all. Instead, he had gone to buy cocaine from a local drug dealer and the man sold him sugar instead. When he got home and realized it was sugar, he went back to get the real thing. The dealer told him that he was neither giving him any more drugs or his money back. My fiancé then attempted to apply his position as an agent by pulling out his badge and gun and a shootout ensued. He jumped into his car and the drug dealer broke his car window. They were shooting at each other. He jumped out of the car and ran for his life as the drug dealer chased him and shot after him. That was not all I learned. I learned that my fiancé had borrowed (and owed) money to just about everyone in his office. He had a serious drug habit.

On my way home I became grossly overwhelmed. I cried and I cried. "Is this really happening, God?" I asked. "Why is this happening to me?" I have to be honest and say that I became angry with God. "I just don't understand it, God. Why are you letting this happen to me? I'm supposed to be getting married. He's supposed to be my husband! And you take away my husband like this? You don't love me, God? You don't love me?" Oh, the tears! Oh, the pain I felt. Oh, the disappointment. God said nothing.

It took several more painful revelations derived through my valiant efforts to prove my commitment to my fiancé and to the wedding that I wanted so badly for me to hear God's answer to my pleas for an explication of why I had to endure this situation. As my tears never ceased, and my heartache lingered, I demanded once more, "Why, God, why did you let this happen to me?" And then in my spirit I received God's response—

God's Answer:

"Why are you acting like you are the victim here when you are clearly the VICTOR? Did you not say to me, 'If it's not right, then show me a sign?' That is exactly what I did. You are sitting here crying over this mess. Imagine if you two had been married and all of this happened. You would have been stuck! Now pick up your head, dry your tears, and move on."

Lesson:

This was in the early phase of my development of my relationship with God. This response from God enlightened me to the notion that the closer I knowingly keep God to me, the closer God sticks to me in ways unbeknownst to me. I encourage you to look at events in your life and identify the presence of God in those events. God is near, and God has our best interest at heart. Sometimes God's answer is, "No." We have to trust that it for our good. When we are in relationship with God, we will be cared for, provided for, and protected very well. It is a testament to God's omniscience and omnipresence. When God has a plan for your life, watch out; God will not let anyone harm you or interfere with God's plan. I praise God for keeping me close to God's bosom. Hallelujah! Amen.

Song:

"Thank You, Lord, for All You've Done for Me" (Walter Hawkins)

It could have been me
Or just another number
With a tragic end
But you didn't see fit
To let none of these things be
Cause everyday, by your power,
You keep on keeping me
Thank you, Lord, for all you've done for me!

Intercessory Prayer

Scripture

"If my people who are called by my name would just humble themselves and pray and seek my face and turn from their wicked ways, then I will hear from heaven and will forgive their sin and heal their land." 2 Chronicles 7:14 (KJV)

This story is merely my own. I don't believe I have ever told my brother, Kevin, how this situation has played out in terms of my prayers and my concerns. But as I have vivid recollection of how it occurred from my standpoint, I will share it with you now.

Ever since he was a child, my second-youngest brother expressed his desire to be a pilot. Airplanes and helicopters were his favorite toys, which was what he received for all his birthday and holiday gifts. I used to watch him play with his planes and listen to him talk about becoming a pilot. I was proud of him for having his dreams; I wanted nothing more for him in his life than to see them realized. He talked about being a pilot so much. So, as we grew up, I bought into his dream. I told everybody of his dream. I could see him as a prestigious pilot, and I just knew he was going to succeed.

In high school he joined the Air Force ROTC as his first step toward his dream. He was so proud of his uniform, and so was I. My heart warmed at the thought of my brother becoming a pilot. He began talking about becoming a pilot in the Air Force.

After, I relocated to Chicago, my brother was preparing to enlist in the Air Force, the next step toward his pilot destination. One day, however, my mother told me on the phone that my brother learned that he could not become a pilot because he wore glasses. Pilots could not wear glasses. My heart sank at the news. I had never talked to my brother about it, but I knew even as disappointed as I felt, my brother's disappointment must have tripled mine. It made me so sad. There was nothing I could do to help; I really wanted to help! As his big sister, I wanted to fix things. However, there was nothing I could do. The only thing I knew to do was to pray. But this was so final. The decision could not be undone. This hurt so badly. My poor brother. I knew I needed to talk to God through my pain, because this one was a major disappointment. So, in tears, I prayed.

Prayer:

"God, please," I said. "Please don't take my brother's dream away. He's just a young man with a dream. You know how badly he wanted to do this. I know he's hurt. Please let my brother fly. God, please, let him fly." I left it alone.

33

God's Answer:

A few conversations later, the topic came up again between my mother and me. I asked how Kevin was doing. Oh, he is so happy," she replied. I was puzzled. "Huh," I said. She continued, "Yes. They told him that even though he did not qualify to be a pilot, he qualified to have a job associated with flying. He enlisted in the Air Force Reserve, and he will be flying overseas as a medic, assisting those who are injured. He gets to be in planes, and he is happy with that."

I was surprised to hear that and let out a big sigh of relief. I immediately remembered the prayer. "Oh," I said. "He's happy? I am so glad to hear that! That is great news! That is simply great news!" We finished our conversation and we hung up. In tears, I immediately prayed a prayer of thanksgiving to God. I began to sing. I couldn't do anything but praise and thank God for just hearing my prayer and blessing my brother so he wouldn't be hurt.

Lesson:

Again, God showed me that God hears me. We have to learn to go to God humbly. I say humbly because I have pondered whether I was too sure that my brother was going to become a pilot. Was I too proud? I had to examine whether I was too braggadocious before the fact. Theoretically speaking, I acted as though I knew what God was going to do, which if I were not careful, would enable me to begin to think I had this God-me relationship in the bag. And I did not. God's ways are not my ways. This fact keeps us humble; if it fails to do so, then God will do something or allow something to happen that will remind us that we are not on equal footing with God. This blessing was not for me personally, but it was in response to intercessory prayer for someone else. God will bless others in response to our prayers for them. Therefore, it is important that we lift each other up in prayer, for the prayers of the righteous avail much.

Another thing we have to learn is to go to God earnestly and pray through our pain, our disappointments, and our tears. Those are the hardest times to even think about praying. But God promises to hear us. When we realize that God indeed has heard us and has answered us, then it is our responsibility, our duty, to give God all the credit for doing so, by praising God and worshipping God. Now, I am not saying that this is the only time to praise and worship God. What I am suggesting, however is that we must give all praise to God for all our blessings, it is our acknowledgment that our God is all-powerful, and it is our confession of our own weakness and need of God's presence in our lives. God will not leave us or forsake us. The more we interact with God through prayer, the more we will hasten to God's throne, and the more we go to God, the more God will reveal God's self to us, and thus the closer we will become to God. It is an awesome assurance.

Rev. Dr. H. Elaine Joyner

Song:

"Thank you, Lord" (Colon Haywood, Jr.)

Thank you, Lord.
Thank you, Lord.
Thank you, Lord.
I just want to thank you, Lord.
I wanna thank you.
I wanna thank you.
I wanna thank you.
Thank you for being good.

Write the Book

Scripture:

"And Jacob was left alone. And a man wrestled with him until the breaking of the day. When the man saw that he did not prevail against Jacob, he touched his hip socket, and Jacob's hip was put out of joint as he wrestled with him. Then he said, "Let me go, for the day has broken." But Jacob said, "I will not let you go unless you bless me." And he said to him, "What is your name?" And he said, "Jacob." Then he said, "Your name shall no longer be called Jacob, but Israel, for you have striven with God and with men, and have prevailed." Then Jacob asked him, "Please tell me your name." But he said, "Why is it that you ask my name?" And there he blessed him. So Jacob called the name of the place Peniel, saying, "For I have seen God face to face, and yet my life has been delivered."

Genesis 32:24-28 (ESV)

Scripture:

"Trust in the Lord with all thine heart; and lean not unto thine own understanding. In all thy ways acknowledge him, and he shall direct thy paths."

Proverbs 3:5-6 (KJV)

When I was young, I found myself in an entanglement. Most people would call it inappropriate, but I had a tough time referring to it as such. Of course, having been young and vulnerable, my train of thought was, "Inappropriate for whom? If it works for me, then that is all that matters." "I mean, if there's someone who's going to sign for my apartment, make the security deposit for my apartment, pay the monthly rent, fully furnish it, plus a stereo system and washer and dryer, pay my car note and insurance, take me out of town on holidays to shop in Atlanta's Lenox Square, showering me with designer suits, jewelry, and purses, spend three and four nights a week at my place, and be there for everything I needed, then that entanglement was inappropriate for whom? Certainly, not me." I had everything I needed. I had everything I wanted. And in my own misguided religiosity, because of my prior relationship with God, I knew that it all had to have been a blessing from God. In fact, I could not have been happier.

But God has a way of straightening us out when we are misguided in our faith and taking wrong turns. God has a way of letting us know when what we are doing is out of the will of God. It is my belief that God will not let us rest easy when God is not pleased with what we're doing, or when God has a plan for our lives, something more for us to do. That Holy Spirit that guides our conscience will not let us rest.

Again, everything was good in my life. I felt good. I lived well. Everything was good! But something inside of me was eating away at me. I did not understand it. I couldn't explain it. My heart felt very heavy. Every Sunday when I came from church, I felt uneasy. I didn't want for anything, but somehow, I wanted more. I had everything, but for some reason, I began to feel that this "everything" was not enough. Why could I not rest? Why was my spirit uneasy? I was already a success. Why, with my having everything, did the life I was living seem insufficient? What was the problem? This uneasiness tore at me day after day. I needed to pray.

I remember hearing my then-pastor, Rev. Dr. Charles B Jackson, Sr., preach a sermon about praying. He told the congregation that when we pray, we should not get up until we hear from God. He assured us that God would answer us; we only had to be persistent in our prayer and to be intentional in our prayer, and to listen for God's answer, because God WILL answer us. During my time of uneasiness that sermon resonated with me. I remember being at church so restless that while in church I could only think of going home, getting on my knees, and following that prescription of prayer that had been asserted by the pastor. I was going to do it. I was going to go home, get on my knees beside my bed, and pray as hard as I could because my soul was not satisfied. I knew how to talk to God. I had done it many times before. So, it was my plan to stay down scratch that it was my plan to talk to God so openly, and clearly, and honestly, and humbly, and wait for God to answer. I intended on hearing an answer from God that day. Church ended. I drove home.

I went inside my apartment in tears. I needed God. I needed to hear from God. I got on my knees. I clasped my hands, rested my elbows on my bed, and with my eyes closed, tears streaming down my face, I began to pray.

Prayer:

"Dear God. I don't know what's wrong. I just know that your girl is uneasy. I just know that you have more for me than this. I am not happy in this, God. Yes, I have every material thing I want. Yes, I have everything I need. Yet still, God, I am not happy. I know that you have more for me than this. I know that you have more for me than this kind of relationship. Forgive me, oh God. I'm sorry for being in this. This is not all I am. This is not all you made me to be. God, you have gifted me, you have blessed me with so many gifts. I have an education and can teach. I am blessed with the gift of song and can sing. You have given me the gift of performance-I can act. And you have blessed me to be able to write, oh God. I remember my mentor telling me that one day I would have to choose one skill and focus on that one, but God, I like them all. Show me which one you want me to do. Tell me which one you want me to do God and I will do it. I want to do your will. I want to do what you want me to do. Tell me, God, which one do I do? Please give me an answer."

The tears continued to stream down my face, as I knelt there in silence. I didn't know what to do, I just knew that I was pouring out my heart to God. So, I stayed there in that position for another few moments with no answer, with nothing happening.

Prayer:

I began speaking again. "God, Pastor Jackson told us to pray, and when we pray, we should not get up until we hear from you. I believe what he said. He told us that you would answer. I am not getting up until I hear from you. God, I'm praying, and I won't get up until you answer me." My tears continued to pour down my face. The spirit was really working with me. I needed guidance from God. I needed a new direction from God. I wanted my life to glorify God. At that time, my life was glorifying me. It wasn't enough. So, I continued, "Which one do you want me to do, God? Please, tell me which one do you want me to do? Do I sing? Do I ask? Do I write? Do I teach? Please, God, tell me what you want me to do."

Still on my knees, weeping, with my head resting on my hands, I waited. I waited for an answer from God. I was determined. I never doubted that God would answer me because the PASTOR said that he would answer me. I was expecting an answer from God that day during that prayer session. Yet, I was hearing nothing. Still resting on the promise of my Pastor, I petitioned the Lord once again, this time more emphatically than ever, and this time looking up to the sky.

Prayer:

"God, I'm not getting up! I'm not getting up until you answer me! Pastor said that you would answer me! So, I'm going to pray, and I won't get up until you answer me!" Oh, the tears! Oh, my desperation! I continued, "I expect you to answer me, God! I need you to answer me!" my weeping was uncontrollable at this point. So, I put my head back down, but this time in the palm of my hands. I cried and I cried, and When I stopped crying, I just stayed there in silence.

God's Answer:

Then, all of a sudden, I heard a voice, a whispering voice say to me, "Write the book," Pleasantly startled, I lifted my head and opened my eyes. I looked up to the heavens and smiled with astonishment. Wow! God had answered me! Just as Pastor had promised! God answered me! Yes, I was taken aback! But God told me loudly and clearly what God had for me to do and what God wanted me to do. And now, 30 years later, after having been afraid to write the book, I present to you this first book, *God, I'm Praying and I Won't Get Up: Establishing and Solidifying a Relationship with God Through Prayer,* a book through which God will get all the glory. I write it with courage, truth, power, and faith in God's word and God's will for my life.

Lesson:

When you are in relationship with God, you can call upon God and insist upon an answer from God. It doesn't have to be an answer that is to your liking, but merely an active response from God. Most of the time we consider God's responses to us in retrospect. We consider after examining on the backend. This story is proof that God will answer you in the midst of your prayers. It also indicates that God will answer us directly and we can count on a response from God. It is OK to be persistent and insistent in prayer. Our relationship with God affords us the prerogative to do so. We are not being disrespectful by holding God to God's word to be there for us whenever we need God, wherever we need God, and however we need God. Establishing a relationship with God is the integral step that enables us to come boldly before God and to God in whatever way we deem necessary to get our point across. Because of our boldness, God will not withdraw God's self from us. Hallelujah to Jesus!

Another lesson I take from this story is when God tells you to do something, do it. God gave me the directive, "Write book" nearly thirty years ago, yet I lived in fear of doing so. If God tells you to do something, there is no room for fear. You do not have to worry about what others will think; you don't have to worry about the ramifications of doing so. When God gives you a directive, know that God will see you all the way through the completion of that directive. No weapon formed against you will prosper. Especially when God has given you the vision. I look back in retrospect and wish I had authored this book long ago. I know that it is going to be a blessing to others and an aid to their formation and/or elevation of their relationship with God. And with that blessing, God will indeed get the glory. Hallelujah to Jesus!

Now that I am following God's directive, I realize that "the book" does not have to be limited to one book. In fact, God has graciously given me five books with five differing objectives that will both help others and glorify God. In doing so, God has provided me with a logical sequence of content that will support the initial manuscript. I am overflowing with excitement because I am now walking in that directive. I give God all praise, honor, and glory for the gift of penmanship that God has given me.

I now am ready to operate outside of my comfort zone and face whatever backlash that may accompany the book, as God's purpose supersedes any fear that I may have had. I have gone thirty years with God's voice in my mind, with God's directive in my mind, ignoring them both. My reluctance to follow God's directive was nothing less than sheer disobedience. However, this book is my first act of obedience regarding writing. I am following what God has told me to do. Hallelujah to God!

Still another lesson is that God is seated high on the throne, yet listening to our every prayer, our every whisper, and in tune to our every concern. I love that we can talk to God in prayer, and that God will literally talk back. This prayer-response event elevates our relationship with God to even higher levels. It certainly has elevated my levels of joy, security, and confidence, as I know I have a God who is really in tune to me. I have a God who really hears me, and who is really there for me. I must stress here that faith plays a significant role in this process. We must go to God believing that God will answer us. I think our belief in the possibility of getting an immediate aural response from God is key to its actual occurrence. Do not go to God in doubt. If you do so, I cannot guarantee or promise your success. I just know the intense level of faith upon which my insistence was based.

So, now, I encourage you to go to God in prayer and ignite or solidify that relationship with God so that you will be emboldened to insist upon God's response to your most immediate request; then watch God show God's faithfulness to you. What is show amazing about the story is that this response is unlike all the other responses from God in this book. It is an immediate response, while all the others were responses examined in retrospect. Try it. Prayer puts you in that position of relationship with God. Talk to God in prayer and do not get up until you actually hear God's answer. Watch your relationship grow.

Song:

"I Can Go to God in Prayer"

Sometimes My Burdens Get So Heavy
(I Can Go To God In Prayer)
He Will Take My Gloom And Sadness
(Turn It In To Light)
Oh, I Can Call Him When I Need Him
Father, Up In Heaven
I Can Go To God In Prayer
I Can Go To God In Prayer

Graduate School:
God Knows Best

Scripture

"Trust in the LORD with all your heart, and do not lean on your own understanding. In all your ways acknowledge him, and he will make straight your paths."

Proverbs 3: 5-6 (ESV)

After having determined that I was going to move out of my home city of Columbia, I knew that I had always wanted to live in the Midwest. I had heard that they were giving out fellowships to African-American students who wanted to go to college at the Big Ten universities. All I had to do was complete one application, and that single application would be used to apply to all the colleges of my choice. I knew that I wanted to be near Oprah Winfrey, so I just picked the colleges in the Midwest. The University of Illinois at Chicago was one of them, as well as Michigan State University. Within a few weeks I received a phone call from the dean of the college of education at Michigan

State. I had been accepted into their doctoral education program. In fact, I had received a full doctoral fellowship to attend Michigan State University education program. I was ecstatic! The Dean told me that I would be receiving further information with further instructions in the coming days and to look out for them.

"I cannot believe it. God really does answer prayer," is what I thought to myself. I praised God. I thanked God for hearing and answering my prayer. And I felt reassured that God was indeed with me. I was just profoundly grateful. I knew nothing about Michigan State University except that it was in the Midwest, so I began my research. I looked up their mascot and found that they were the Wolverines. I told people at my church and my family that I was moving to Michigan to become a Michigan State Wolverine. I was so excited. Plus, I knew I was getting my Doctorate degree. I was going to be like my pastor with a Doctorate degree, and I was going to earn it. I could not be prouder of myself.

Within a few days, just as the dean had explained, I received an envelope from the school. I was so excited to open it. This was the beginning of my new life. When I opened the envelope, I began reading the letter. I found that it was not a letter with further instructions as I had anticipated. Instead, it was a letter advising me that the offer, the fellowship to Michigan State University had been rescinded. "What?" I said to myself. I kept reading. The letter continued with we are sorry to inform you, but we cannot offer you the fellowship into the program the education program at Michigan State University at this time. You do not have the pre-requisite degree to be allowed into this program. It is required that you have a

Master's degree for entrance into the doctoral program here at Michigan State University. We apologize it was indeed our oversight. We will hold this fellowship for you until after you have completed the Master's program at Michigan State and then you will receive your fellowship. Thank you for understanding, and please pardon our error. We look forward to working with you in the future.

What a shock! What a disappointment! I could not believe it. Utter devastation! I had made a fool out of myself by telling everybody I was going to Michigan State. I would not be going anywhere. I did not have the money to pay for a master's degree. I was just so disappointed. I could not understand why God would let me get to such a high emotionally, only to have me feel let down by such disappointing news.

What was I supposed to learn from this? I have always looked at experiences as learning experiences or teachable moment sent and I pondered what was I to learn from that experience. I could not find anything to learn because I have not done anything wrong. I had followed procedures in my application, I had received affirmation of my acceptance, only to have it taken back from me. I don't know what I was to learn from that. So, yes, I cried. I did. Tearfully, I went to God in prayer, asking God why he would do that to me.

Prayer:

"Dear God, why? Why would you allow me to be accepted, and then remove the acceptance? I am extremely disappointed, Now, I am going to be the laughingstock of the town. Please, God. Please help me get through this, help me get through this hurt and shame. In Jesus' name, I pray.

Amen." I just didn't understand. I told God that I just felt so
hurt. I just felt so hurt. Then I took a deep breath and arose
from my prayer—numb. This one was hard. What was I
going to do now?

God's Answer:

The very next day, I came home from work and found
another letter in my mailbox. This letter was from the
University of Illinois at Chicago. I didn't really want to
open it because I just didn't want any more bad news. I
didn't want to hear another false promise, or any mor
disappointment. I opened it anyway. Much to my surprise,
it was a letter informing me that I have been accepted into
the performing arts program at the University of Illinois at
Chicago; it was a master's program! I could not believe it! I
was receiving yet another fellowship and was to start school
in Chicago in two-and-a-half weeks. "God, is this you
again?" I spoke. "Is this for real?" I could not believe that
I was going to get a Master's in the performing arts from
a university in Chicago! I loved acting. This one felt more
real. It felt more exciting because I was going to be doing
what I wanted to do and loved doing. I did not run and tell
so many people this time. I wanted to make sure that it was
real. Plus, I had only two-an-a-half-weeks to prepare to get
out of my apartment, get packed up, and get prepared to go
off to college.

The transition process went way more smoothly than
I ever could have imagined. I had made it known that I
was looking for someone to sublet my apartment because
the program was only a year long. I knew that I would be
returning to Columbia. I did not, however, have any idea

of where I would stay in Chicago. Chicago was a huge city. I needed to stay someplace safe, but where? I had no knowledge of anyone who live there. I did not know anything.

A friend of mine had a friend who was looking for an apartment. She came over and looked at my apartment. I told her she could use everything in the apartment. What she said next was amazing. She told me that her grandmother lived in Chicago and said that I could come and live with her for a nominal fee. And as long as I was in college, I could stay with her. God was amazing! I knew that this was God at work. That is the only way I could have gotten this done in two weeks' time and been in my car and driving up to Chicago. Everything went off without a hitch. The young lady moved into my apartment. I moved in with her grandmother and began my journey, my academic journey in Chicago. What I felt at the time after the big disappointment initially and what I still feel is that when God is at work you know it. When God's hand is in something you know it. I did not qualify for the other program. However, I thought that with that first disappointment, there was no hope.

Lesson:

God knew what I needed even when I did not know. Sometimes we won't understand God's ways. We simply must trust God... In ALL things. I did not need to be in Michigan. I knew nobody there. God had already worked things out for me in Chicago. The transitions on both ends were easy. I had someone to sublet my apartment and I was able to be housed, enrolled, and in class in two-and-a-half weeks. God is amazing. My trust in and dependence upon God grew even stronger. I could feel God's love and care for me. God will never leave us or forsake us. We must trust in that promise as righteous children of God. My Chicago Pastor taught us that "delay does not mean denial." That was the lesson that I took from that experience—Delay does not mean denial. God had answered my prayer. "Baby, I'm still here. I am still in control. I got you." The reassurance was amazing. Hallelujah to Jesus!

Song:

"I've Never Seen the Righteous Forsaken" (Donald Lawrence and the Tri-City Singers)

I Was Young, And Now I'm Old,
Seen A Lot Of Situations Unfold.
Been A Lot Of Places,
Met All Kinds,
But There's One thing That Stays On My Mind:
Out Of All The Things I've Done,
And The Things I've Seen.
I've Never Seen The Righteous Forsaken.

Keep You from Falling

Scriptures:

"For I, the LORD thy God will hold thy right hand, saying unto thee, Fear not; I will help thee." Isaiah 41:13 (KJV)

"I was pushed hard, so that I was falling, but the LORD helped me. The LORD is my strength and my song; he has become my salvation." Psalm 118:13-14 (ESV)

When I moved to Chicago, I made frequent trips back home to South Carolina. I loved going home. Home gave me a sense of belonging. So, every chance I got, I went home. Sometimes I flew, and other times, I drove. Whenever I flew, I looked for the cheapest flight I could find. Cheaper airlines had started to pop up with unbelievable values, but the cheap fares often required an alternate airport, as opposed to flying straight into Columbia. I chose a flight from Greenville, South Carolina, because of its affordability. I had no problem renting a car and driving about ninety miles to get home to Columbia because I knew I was saving a lot of money. This trip had a Mother's Day focus. I wanted to travel home to be with my mom. With it being mid-spring, thunderstorms were a common occurrence.

It was Sunday and I was returning to Chicago's O'Hare airport. The weather was sunny when I left my mom's, but as I drove to the airport, rain began to fall. By the time I arrived at the airport, it was raining profusely. The flight had been delayed a couple of times because of the rain. However, I had to work the next day, and really needed to get back to Chicago.

After a couple of hours, we were cleared to travel. Boy, was I glad! We boarded the plane. It was a small plane, with about twenty to thirty rows of two seats on each side of the aisle. It had a low height clearance which caused tall people to have to bend to walk through I had an aisle seat in the first row behind first class. I sat next to a Caucasian woman stopped reading her book to greet me when I sat down. I had grown very tired and planned to fall asleep once we had taken off. As usual, we were greeted by the Captain over the speaker system. He apologized for the delay and informed us that it was due to the weather; while it was merely raining where we were, there were severe thunderstorms throughout the Midwest, which prevented us from earlier takeoff. He explained that some of the storms had subsided, and therefore, we could fly around them.

Whenever I flew, I made sure to offer up a prayer of supplication, asking God to keep the plane safe throughout the flight, if it was God's will to do so. I never failed to offer that prayer, and this time was no different. "Dear God, please give us safe travel to Chicago, if it is your will. In the name of Jesus, I pray. Amen," I prayed. Then I closed my eyes to rest.

As we began to taxi, I looked across the woman and out of the window to see the rain still falling, and I could see some lightning down the way, verifying the storms of which the captain spoke. I believed that we were okay because the captain said that we were okay. But I uttered my prayer again— "God, please keep us safe. Amen."

The takeoff was pretty smooth. Again, I glanced over my neighbor to see what appeared to be a storm down the way. I was glad we were not going that way and didn't have to go through that. We ascended normally. We had not leveled off for even three minutes when suddenly, we encountered extreme turbulence. It was the worst turbulence I had ever experienced, for we were bouncing high and roughly, and I became scared. I glanced through my peripheral at my neighbor to see if she wanted to say something or if she was afraid. She just kept holding her book with two hands and pretending as though she was reading (you will never convince me that this woman wasn't anxious because this turbulence was extreme). The strength she modeled was admirable, though. Because this level of turbulence was new to me, I viewed her behavior as standard and sought to pattern myself after her. I looked at a man across the aisle from me. He was calm, but he wore his fear in his sleeve, for his eyes were clenched tightly, he was squeezing the outside armrest, and his face was red as apples. He was a big man, too. I knew he was afraid.

The turbulence continued. We kept bouncing and bouncing. The plane kept wobbling and wobbling. You could hear it squeaking as it wobbled. "Oh, my God," I thought to myself. "When is it going to stop?" I looked at the woman; I looked at the man. They both still had the same demeanors. I was about ready to scream. I could feel the plane climbing. The captain told us that he was going to try to fly over this one. We were climbing and flying amazingly fast, faster than I could remember ever having flown before. I was so scared. I couldn't fight it anymore. The tears began to fall.

Bumpety, bumpety, bump! Bumpety, bumpety, bump! Squeak, squeak, squeak, squeak! That is all I remember. For miles, for minutes, what felt like forever! I glanced at the woman. She had put her book away. Tears were streaming down my face by that time. I couldn't stop them. And then the unthinkable happened. Suddenly, all the plane's power went off. Silence... No motor... No turbulence... no sound. The plane began to drop... like straight down. We were just dropping. We were just dropping! I looked at the woman. This time she looked at me. She too was crying. She grabbed my hand. I began to pray again through my tears.

Prayer:

"Oh, God, please. Don't let this plane crash. Please, God, please., don't let this plane crash! Whatever I've done, I'm sorry, Lord. Please don't let this plane crash! If you don't want me to fly anymore, I won't fly, but please don't let this plane crash! Please, God, please! Help us, please...!"

God's Answer:

After about thirty-five to forty seconds of silent dropping, the plane suddenly jerked, and power was restored. The motor was back on; the lights were back on. We were flying again! It was smooth, it was quiet. We all sat still. Very still. I wiped my face. My neighbor wiped her face. She grabbed her book and continued to read. I, again prayed, but this time it was a prayer of thanksgiving. I told God, "Thank-you" so many times! I expressed my love and gratitude and reverence to God.

When we landed at the airport in Chicago, the whole plane erupted in a roaring applause! Woo-hoo! Yeah! Yes! Yes! Yes! We were all so incredibly happy to be on the ground! I knew that it was only because of God that we landed safely. I give God all the praise for my life. Glory to God!

Lesson:

As a child I often heard it said that "God will never let you fall." This plane incident serves as a literal example of this comforting assertion. But what it does is it proves that we can take God figuratively and literally. I just remember the grown folks saying that "God will keep you from falling." We often find ourselves at wit's end, about to bottom out. When we call on the name of the Lord, God is faithful and just to hear our every cry. God heard me that day! Hallelujah! Hallelujah for God's grace! Hallelujah for God's mercy! Hallelujah for God's love! God hears us and God knows us, and when we are in despair, God is right there, never forsaking the righteous! Whenever you find yourself in trouble, call God immediately. Hasten to his throne. And God will hear your cry, pity your groan, and keep you from falling.

Song:

"I Love the Lord" (Whitney Houston)

I love the Lord
He heard my cry
And pitied every groan
Lon as I live
And troubles rise
I'll hasten to his throne

Song:

"In the Midst of It All" (Yolanda Adams/Written by Kevin Bond)

Not because I've been so faithful
Not Because I've always obeyed
It's not because I trust him
To be with me all of the way
But it's because He loves me so dearly
He was there to answer my call
There always to protect me
For He's kept me in the midst of it all

HE WOKE ME UP THIS MORNING, AND STARTED ME ON MY WAY

Scripture:

"Are not five sparrows sold for two pennies? And not one of them is forgotten before God. Why, even the hairs of your head are al numbered. Fear not; you are of more value than many sparrows." Luke 12: 6-7 (ESV)

I used to hear "The Lord is Blessing Me " sung in church on Sunday mornings. It was one of my favorite hymns. I have to say, however, that I believed they were singing about everyone's general morning awakening. There was much to be thankful for in just the general awakening, for it did not have to occur. God could have chosen another way for each one of us. So, whenever the choir sang that line, I sang it with fervor because I was glad that it had not gone another way. I was glad to be alive.

It wasn't until I had relocated to Chicago in pursuit of my first Master's degree that I was able to witness first-hand God physically waking me from my sleep. It was an experience of which I still stand in awe, and that I will cherish for the rest of my life.

It was the day I was to defend my Master's thesis. I had stayed up studying until the wee hours of the morning the night before, so needless to say, when I decided to turn in, I was very tired. I knew I had to wake up early, however, to beat the traffic, for my defense was at 8:00 the next morning. Rush-hour traffic in Chicago is horrendous at that time of morning. I could not be late It was especially important for me to get up in time to make it to the school. So, before I went to bed, I prayed and asked God to let me not oversleep the next day.

Prayer

"God," I prayed. "Please don't let me oversleep and miss my defense. Amen." I went to sleep.

God's Answer:

The next morning, as I slept on my stomach, I was awakened by a repeated tapping sensation on the small of my lower back. It felt like some was twiddling their fingers, as if tapping on a desk. I woke up and looked around, but no one was there. I looked at the clock and it was exactly an hour-and-a half before I was due at school. I knew it was God. As I went to take a shower and passed my roommate's room, I looked in found that she was still asleep. It could not have been her. So, I just told God' Thank you," for I knew God had again answered my prayer. It was then that the generalized testament that, "He woke me up this morning, and started me on my way," became my personal testimony.

Lesson:

God is so amazing. God awakened me personally and physically with God's own touch. God's omnipresence, his ability to be everywhere, is real! Yes, God is a big God, but not too big to attend to each one of us. God cares for each one of us. God will answer your smallest utterance. When you trust God, God will show God's faithfulness to us. And when God does, we must not forget to give God all the credit and praise. This was yet another beautiful blessing to me from God, and another indication that God and I really are in relationship, that God is really nearby and present for me and you. I am still humbled at the thought. Hallelujah to Jesus!

Song:

"For Every Mountain" (Kurt Carr)

For waking me up this morning
That's why I praise you
For starting me on my way
That's why I praise you
For letting me see the sunshine
Of a brand-new day
For brand new mercies
Along with each new day

"The Lord is Blessing Me" (Bishop Larry Trotter and Sweet Holy Spirit)

The Lord is blessing me
Right now, right now, right now.
The Lord is blessing me
Right now, right now, right now.
He woke me up this morning
And started me on my way.
The Lord, the Lord, the Lord
Is blessing me -e-e right now.

"Order My Steps"

Scriptures:

"Do not be anxious about anything, but in everything by prayer and supplication let your requests be made known to God." Philippians 4:6 (ESV)

"The steps of a man are established by the Lord, when he delights in his way;"

Psalm 37:23 (ESV)

"The heart of man plans his way, but the Lord establishes his steps." Proverbs 16:9 (ESV)

"The steps of a man are established by the Lord, when he delights in his way; though he fall, he shall not be cast headlong, for the Lord upholds his hands." Psalm 37: 23-24 (ESV)

"For I know the plans I have for you, declares the Lord, plans for welfare and not for evil, to give you a future and a hope." Jeremiah 29: 11(ESV)

I had just completed a one-year master's degree program at the University of Illinois at Chicago, but upon completing the degree, I was not ready to go back home to South Carolina, where I would pick up where I had left off as a third-grade teacher. I kind of liked Chicago; there was so much to do there. It was such an amazing city. Besides, I had dreams of becoming an entertainer, and what better place to test the waters? But time was running out for me to make a decision. I needed to know what I was going to do. My employer in Carolina needed to know if the needed to hold my position. This was causing me much anxiety.

One thing I knew was that I needed to make it through the summer and by that, I mean financially. I knew that that because of the teaching profession's adaptability and availability, I could get a teaching job somewhere in the fall; so, if I could just make it through the summer, then I would be okay. As I was an actor, and had performed in plays in Columbia, I researched nearby local theaters in Chicago to see if there were any upcoming summer productions for which I could audition. I learned of an audition that was coming up for a play, "God's Trombones," at a local theater. I pondered the notion of auditioning for it. I could use the money I made from it to pay my rent and car payment for the summer, and then I could stay. However, I wanted to make sure that God wanted me to stay. I needed God to tell me if it was in God's will for me to stay. So, I did what I had always done— I consulted God in prayer.

Prayer:

"God," I said. "I'm not ready to go home. I'm sure I can get a teaching job here in the fall, but I need money to carry me through the summer. There is a play coming up that I want to audition for. The money I'd make from it will take me through the summer. I don't know whether I'll get cast in the play or not, though. So, God, my question is, 'Do I try to stay here, unsure of what's going to happen, or do I go home where I know I have a job?' You know what's best for me. Please help me decide. I trust you, God. I know what I want, but please tell me what you want for me. If you want me to stay, then let me land a role in this play. If I don't land a role in the play, then I will know that you want me to go home. Whatever happens, I will accept it as your will. I trust you to carve my path. In the name of Jesus I pray, Amen."

It was at that moment that I decided that I was going to step out on faith and try to stay. I was going to audition for the play, "God's Trombones," and put my entire future in the hands of God. It was a faith move, for I had absolutely no idea how things would turn out but had decided to accept whatever the turn-out was as God's will for my life. I had prayed, telling God my concerns and desires; I concluded my prayer with a declarative deal describing my role and God's role- "God, I'm going to audition for this play. You know what I want. But if it's not what you think I should do, then I'll accept that. If I land a role, then I'll know you want me to stay. If I don't, then I'll know you want me to go home."

God's Answer:

I auditioned for the play and got the part. Immediately, I thanked God. I was surprised at how God heard my prayer and answered me. My anxiety disappeared. I felt a profound sense of peace, for I knew I served a God who hears me, loves me, answers me, and who is always so near to me. I have been in Chicago over twenty-eight years now. I give all praise to God for God's sustenance over the years; for God's safekeeping during my over seventy solo drives to Carolina and back, I praise God!

Lesson:

This story is not merely exemplary of God's faithfulness, or of God answering prayer, but it also is one that exemplifies relationship between the prayer (one who prays) and God. God is establishing relationship as God answers our prayer, for God is showing, "Yes, I am here. Yes, I am real; yes, you can trust me, and yes, I have your back. Just trust me and believe in me and my power, and I will be there for you." When one trusts, believes, and relies upon another, one is participating in a trusting relationship. As one who prays, you can base your expectation and reliance upon God based upon your prior interactions with God, and upon God's blessings. In my past, God has proven God's-self to be nearby, to hear me, and to care about me, my needs, and even my wants, much like a close friend, but to a much deeper degree.

When God answers our prayers, God is acknowledging and solidifying our relationship with God. God made known to me God's omniscience, omni-presence, and omnipotence. This knowledge I rely upon now and will continue to rely upon all the days of my life. Consult God in all that you do. That is an important component when solidifying your relationship with God.

Rev. Dr. H. Elaine Joyner

Song:

"Order My Steps"

Humbly I ask Thee, teach me Thy will.
While You're working, help me keep still.
Though Satan is busy, God is real.
Order my steps in Your Word.
Please, Order my steps in Your Word.

More Than I Could
Ever Imagine...

Scripture:

"Now unto him who is able to do exceeding abundantly, above all we can ask or think, according to the power that works in us."

Ephesians 3:20 (KJV)

When one hears the Scriptures, one may not immediately apply them to one's life. However, when one discovers how the scriptures align with one's life, the revelation is so astounding that one cannot help but praise God. One cannot help but give God all honor. That is what I did in this situation, it is what I continue to do every time I think about it.

I was in my last year of seminary at the Chicago Theological Seminary. I had not been extremely active on campus, as I had a pretty busy schedule which was comprised of working and going to school; however, something compelled me to want to do something meaningful before I graduated. I was about to graduate from a seminary-something that I never thought would be happening to me. And the realization inspired me to want to do something that would be memorable for me on this ministry journey. Traditionally, students were given the opportunity to lead worship on Wednesdays. Over the course of four years, I had never signed up, because I was afraid. But for some reason I mustered up the courage. I decided that I wanted to lead a worship service. There weren't many worship services left in the year, for we were already heading toward February. So, I dared to sign up for the Ash Wednesday service. I was teaching and directing a choir at my place of employment, and I knew that I would have to somehow join the two together in order to be able to be present at that service.

I was responsible for planning the entire service. This included securing the musician, securing the people to impose the ashes alongside me, imposing the ashes, preaching the sermon, and designing the Ash Wednesday service. Because I had access to my choir, I planned a field trip for them to serve as a choir at the worship service. Lunch always followed the service, so I was able to make sure that the children were fed in addition to blessing the CTS community with their beautiful vocals. It was going to be an African-American History-Ash Wednesday service.

I wrote a sermon entitled, "How Do You Handle Questions?" It was a sermon that arose out of my own experience. It was a sermon I had prayed over and toiled over. I sought to follow Reverend Dr. Frank Thomas' template of preaching, which included the elements of situation, complication, resolution, and celebration. I just wanted to do a good job.

On the day of the worship service, I was a nervous wreck. I went to the school, gathered up the children, got them dressed in their African garb, and headed over to the seminary where they were set to perform as special guests. While it all went off without a hitch, I was still, however, I very insecure about it all. I was about to lead a worship service before my colleagues. I was humbled to no end. I was nervous to no end. After we arrived and I got the kids situated, I went into a private space. I was so overwhelmed by the task, I was so overwhelmed at the notion of standing before my colleagues with a message, I was so overwhelmed by my lack of confidence in my ability as a minister, that I cried for about ten minutes. I cried and prayed to God:

Prayer:

"God, please, don't let me make a fool out of myself before my colleagues."

I was not confident in my knowledge of theology. I was not confidence in my clarity of my theology. So, I didn't want to stand up there and say something that was just all wrong. I just didn't want to do that. I had secured all the help I needed. I had secured the music. I had secured the musician. And I had written the sermon. But I didn't know whether what I had written was good enough, was accurate enough, or would even make sense. Truth told, that's why I never volunteered to do this before. I was terrified. When you talk about humility hi felt lower than everybody else in the room, because I was not confident in my level of intelligence on theology. "So, please God, don't let me make a fool out of myself in front of my colleagues. Amen."

God's Answer:

The service was beautiful. The children were beautiful—they sang to the glory of God, and they sang from their hearts. Thus, they warmed the hearts of all present. Now, I have to say, mind you, that I had to stop in the middle of my sermon a couple of times to get them in order, as they were young kids, but it all goes with the territory. I delivered my sermon we imposed the ashes, we said the final prayer, and it was time for the those in attendance to come and greet the speaker. I asked my friends how it went. Did I do OK? Was it OK? They all answered affirmatively; but they were my friends – they probably said that to be nice.

As the greeting line dwindled the last person to come up and greet me was the president of the seminary. First, she thanked me for such a beautiful service. I humbly said, "You're welcome." She went on to thank me for the message. She said that it was very powerful. Again, I thanked her. But what she said next was astounding. She asked me if I had planned to enter that message in the preaching contest. I told her that I had not planned to enter that message in the preaching contest. And she said to me," I think you should enter that message in the preaching contest." These big eyes of mine grew even bigger as I smiled and said, "OK, I will do that. Thank you so much." She shook my hand and left. My only thought at the time was, "Wow, the president of the seminary just gave me some very warm affirmations. What an honor!" In my mind, and in my heart, I felt that if I had never received another blessing at the school, I had received the ultimate blessing.

I entered the sermon in the preaching contest and WON the Graham Taylor Preaching Award Scholarship! OH, my goodness! I could not believe it! My first response was, "God, for real? You bless me like this? I asked you not to let me make a fool of myself and you bless me like this?" And that was when Ephesians 3 came into play in my life. I was worried about looking silly and God has blessed me way above what I asked I thought about planning that final Ash Wednesday service for me.

And if that wasn't enough, I called Rev. Dr. Frank Thomas, my preaching instructor, to share my good news and thank him for the model of preaching that he asserted. Dr. Thomas was then co-founder and co-publisher of the *African American Pulpit* minister's journal. It was a national journal read by most African Americans in ministry. Dr. Thomas asked me to send him a copy of my sermon. I obliged. Within a couple of weeks, he called me to inform me that he was going to publish the sermon in the journal. What!?! My sermon, published in the *African American Pulpit*?! No way! God, you are really showing out! I sent him a brief bio along with a picture, and my sermon was indeed published in the 2004 Winter Seminarians' edition. God is so good!

And if that wasn't enough, my sermon, "How Do You Handle Questions? "was posted and remained on the website of Chicago Theological Seminary as the sample sermon link to the homepage for the next two years! Hallelujah! Glory to God! "According to the power that works in us." Give God a try. Give... God ...a...try!

Lesson:

When you have a relationship with God, and you put God first in all things, God is faithful and won't disappoint. In fact, when you entrust everything about you to the Lord's guidance and the Lord's hands, there is no way but up. Inasmuch as we elevate God, God elevates us. He is just faithful like that. He is just that kind of God.

When I reflect on this story, I realize that my mere desire to do the work of the Lord at the seminary and do it with my whole heart and in a way that glorifies God was a point, according to the scripture, at which God could find approval. God wants us to let God be our foremost desire. God wants us to let our desire to fulfill God's will or edify God to be the first and foremost thing in our hearts. And when that desire arose in me, I believe that it pleased God. That desire was real. That desire to edify God and do well in the name of Jesus and on behalf of God was real, and I believe God was pleased with that. And God took it way beyond what I had ever considered to be possible.

God "is able to do exceeding abundantly above all we can ask or think according to the power that worketh in us." Now when I think about that part — "according to the power that works in me," I can't help but to give God glory, because if all these amazing blessings arose from a sermon that I crafted according to power that's within me, then their magnitude must indicate that I must have some kind of power in me. We all do. God's word says so. Power that I don't even know about. And that is key. You must tap into your power. The power that works in you revolves around that thing that you are good at. Tap into it. Use it to the glory of God and watch God work. I tell you what I know, firsthand. I don't know why God has chosen me, but I know that God has chosen me. God has gifted me with various abilities. I will use each one to edify God. I urge you to nurture your relationship with God through prayer, and let God lead the way. What if I had not uttered that prayer to God and told God the desires of my heart? We must talk to God in prayer. That is the key to God knowing what we feel inside of us and where we are coming from.

We oftentimes don't even imagine how far or how big things can get for us. We can't even imagine how well we can do or how things can blossom and blossom and blossom. But God knows. Trust God with your life. Communicate with God in prayer, through prayer. Establish that solidified relationship with God through your prayer communication. And watch God work. Amen. Glory to God. Glory to God.

Song:

He's Able (Darwin Hobbs)

Exceedingly, abundantly, above all,
All you could ask or think
According to the power that work it in You, you
God is able to do just what he said he would do
He's gonna fulfill every promise to you
Don't give up on God cause he won't give up on you

GOD'S GOT YOU—GOD GAVE ME MORE TIME

Scripture:

"I have been young and now am old, yet I have not seen the righteous forsaken, nor his children begging for bread." Psalms 37:25 (ESV)

I could tell that the end of my marriage was near. It was just a feeling I had. We'd had disagreements before, but this one was different. I felt it in my core. My marriage was over. While I had great concern about living on my own, I didn't panic. I immediately thought of what I could do to help myself. "I could become an administrator and increase my income," I thought to myself. "But that means going back to school another year-and-a-half. And I might not have that much time. Man, I just finished getting my second Master's degree two months ago. That was four years of school. I really don't feel like going back to school. What am I going to do?" And then I decided, "I'm just gonna have to go for it. Even though I just graduated two months ago, I must get this degree in administration. I'm gonna do it."

At that very point of making my decision, I uttered a prayer to God,

Prayer:

"God, please hold the divorce off until I can get this degree and make more money to support myself. Amen."

I enrolled in school in the fall of 2004, completed the program in March of 2006, and graduated and became certified in May of 2006. My divorce became final in May of that same year, and I began my assistant-principalship on July 1, 2006. I give God all glory and praise!

I cannot tell this story without going into detail about and giving God the glory for the Assistant Principal position. When I first started the program, my principal approached me about becoming her assistant principal upon graduation, for her then Assistant Principal planned to retire in 2006. Of course, I accepted the offer and was ecstatic. At that point, I knew God's hand was in the mix. However, as the time drew near to my graduation, job politics and chatter indicated that the principal had changed her mind and had opted to go in a different direction— to appoint a friend who had neither training nor certification. However, she had named me Lead Teacher and sent me to another series of training sessions. I was devastated. I cried and yelled at God a little bit, saying,

Prayer:

"God, I thought you had me on this! I thought you were with me! You know I need this position. You know I'm getting a divorce! You know what I asked. You know how hard I've worked. And you just leave me like this? What am I going to do now?" The school year ended, and I went home sad, anxious, defeated, and bewildered.

God's Answer:

About three days into my summer vacation, I received what was then a secret call from my friend, who was the clerk at the school. I thought she was merely calling to check on me because she knew how disappointed I'd been. However, she was laughing and giggling. When I asked her what was going on, she stated, "I'm just so tickled, I don't know what to do! You are going to be offered that AP position." "Huh," I responded. "Yes! The board said that she could not put someone who is not qualified in that position, so she is going to give it to you!" "You are lying," I said. I began to scream. Oh, my God! God you are so amazing!" And she said, "Look at God!" We praised God for a good fifteen minutes before we got to the order of business. Then she continued, "I'm calling to see if you can come in on Monday to meet with her." "Well, Yeah," I replied. I will see you then. We hung up the phone and I just prayed a prayer of apology and thanksgiving to God. God, you really do have me! Thank you so much! You never cease to amaze me! Please forgive me. I was simply scared. I love you, Lord, and give you all the praise. Glory to your name! Amen."

Lesson: When you utter your prayer in faith, trust that God hears you. I remembered my prayer that I had offered to God over a year-and-a-half earlier. But when the powers and principalities got busy and attempted to do what they do—tried to make me lose my faith, in my desperation,

I wondered if God had forgotten me. In fact, I thought that maybe this was not God's plan for me and my life's path. But since I neither knew what the path was, nor did I know God's plan, I panicked and blamed God. As usual, God came through, like God had done so many times. I'd enrolled in school in the fall of 2004, completed the program in a year-and-a-half (by March, 2006). I became certified in May of 2006, and my divorce became final in May of that same year. Then, God blessed me to begin my assistant-principalship a month later, on July 1, 2006. Everything went like clockwork I give God all glory and praise! How could I have doubted? I felt so ashamed about my behavior. I repented and asked God for forgiveness. We must learn to trust that God is as faithful as God has always been, even in our most vulnerable times, for God won't let us down. God's got me and God's got you.

Song:

So You Would Know (Brooklyn Tabernacle Choir)

CHORUS
Didn't I wake you up this morning
Were you clothed in your right mind
When you walked on this problem
Didn't I step right in on time
When you got weak along life's journey
My angel carried you
So you would know just how much I love you

Guardian Angel

Scripture:

"Have I not commanded you? Be strong and courageous. Do not be frightened, and do not be dismayed, for the LORD your God is with you wherever you go." Joshua 1: 9 (ESV)

I had lived in Chicago about eighteen years. As we all know, Chicago has gotten increasingly more dangerous over time. I had encountered a couple of dangerous situations, myself, as was groped while leaving a movie theater with my husband and stepson and followed home after having worked a moonlighting job with a band. Carrying a weapon in public was illegal there at the time, so did not have a gun, nor did I want one. However, I could carry mace. So I did some research on what type of mace would work best for me and found a brand called "Guardian Angel." The name, itself, caught my attention. I believe in angels and believe that they are designed to watch over and protect God's people. Thus, the name was befitting for the purpose for which I needed it. I needed to feel safe. I needed to feel protected and watched over.

This mace was deemed to be so potent that it would cause serious harm to the skin upon contact. It promised to ward away attackers instantly. When inhaled, it purported to make attackers turn away just to catch their breath. The Guardian Angel had other attractive components such as a horizontal trigger position (which made it posture like a gun). I was sold at its potency.

While I received the package with great anticipation, I hoped that I never had to use it. I knew, however that if I ever found myself in another vulnerable situation, I would be ready. I knew that I would be well-protected because I had my "Guardian Angel." In fact, every time I left my home and grabbed my mace, I stated that I felt secure because I had my "Guardian Angel" mace. I knew I was going to be safe outside because I was protected. I carried it wherever I went, whenever I left home.

I'd had the "Guardian Angel" for about six months and had never used it, so I was concerned about whether it was working properly. I decided to do a test shot to determine its functionality. I held it sideways and aimed it like a gun. When I pulled the trigger, boy, did it startle me. It did not spray like other mace sprays, but instead it made a poof-like popping sound, and I saw a ball of gas shoot quickly across the parking lot. Although I had shot it away from myself, I could smell the gas from its fumes. I began to cough. I concluded that it still worked. Six months later, I repeated the test run and again concluded that my "Guardian Angel" was indeed working properly. I carried my angel wherever I went for another two years.

One day when my husband and I were walking to the car, I remembered that I had not tested the "Guardian

Angel" out in a while. So I began telling him about how powerful it was, and how toxic it was. I bragged on how it would burn the face of my assailant instantly, and I could just run away. I talked about how it shot like a gun and not like those little pepper sprays. Then, I asked him to watch as I demonstrated it. I told him to stand back because I did not want him to be affected by the fumes. "Are you ready," I asked. "Cause here goes..." I aimed... Pulled... And... NOTHING! "What?," I exclaimed, as I examined the gadget. And oh, boy, did my husband start laughing. "Okay, 'Guardian Angel,' he said. That's some protection!" Oh, he could not stop laughing. Puzzled by its malfunction, I looked at it, twisted it, and turned it. I had spent over fifty dollars on this thing, and you mean it's not working? I tested it twice and it was working; now it won't do anything! Oh, I'm calling the manufacturer. They are going to hear from me," I asserted. My husband just continued to laugh. "You thought that thing was protecting you and it did NOTHING!" "Oh, my gosh," I said. "What if something had happened? I would have been standing there, pointing this stupid thing, and my attacker would have just gotten me." "Oh, my! Let me go look up this product and get with the manufacturer because this thing is truly defective.

I rushed to my computer, found the product, and read its specifications. What I found was astounding. I learned that the "Guardian Angel Mace" contained only two shots... and I had used both up in test shots. "Oh, wow! What a fool I'd been," I thought to myself. "I have been walking around with this gadget thinking I was protected, and it had nothing in it! Nothing at all." My heart began racing at my thoughts of the potential harm that could have come to me as I relied on that mace and pointed that it at someone only for it to fail because I had used up its contents.

Then the Holy Spirit spoke to me— I had carried that can of mace with me wherever I went, and it could do nothing. I had put all my trust in a product that could do nothing; and yet, no harm came to me. A can of mace can't keep me from harm; only God can. God is the real Guardian Angel who was there with me. God had protected me. My safety does not reside in a can. My safety resides in God. God is my Guardian Angel who was with me all along.

Prayer:

God, please forgive me. I put all my confidence in product, a product that has no power. You are my sole Guardian Angel. You kept me safe in spite of me, despite my foolish thinking. I am nothing without you. I do not deserve your goodness, but I praise you. Thank you for your love. God, from this day forward I will remember to give you praise in all things. You are the ONE. No matter what happens, God, it's you. You are the one. In the name of Jesus, I pray. Amen.

Lesson:

This lesson is a simple one. Do not put your trust in anything but God. God is in everything, and God is everything. We must put our trust in God. Even if we acquire a gadget of sorts, we must still realize that God is the ultimate source of our existence. Unintentionally, I put my trust in the mace. We are safe because of God. We are protected because of God. We got this gadget because of God. God ids with us wherever we go. To put our trust in a material object models idolatry. Putting our faith in God means putting our faith in God in all things. As believers, that is what we must do. God has our back, even when we do not know that we need it. Hallelujah to the Lord!

Song:

He Was There All the Time (Rev. James Moore)

When I felt like giving up
He was there all the time
He was there all the time
Waiting patiently in light
The Lord was there
The Lord was there
Jesus was there
All the time

A Bad Decision: God Restored Me

Scripture:

"Great is our Lord, and abundant in power. His understanding is beyond measure."
Psalm 147:5 (ESV)

According to my former, Pastor, we are to choose mates with whom we have a lot in common. We ought to choose mates who believe in the same God as we, for it is essential that we are equally yoked. I did not do that, however, in choosing my husband, who was of a different faith. When I asked him how we were going to do a relationship as people of differing faiths, he replied that, "We were going to be the example." I loved the notion, and jumped right in.

Things went well, at first. I visited the mosque (but was turned away), and he visited my place of worship several times. He recognized my holidays, and I recognized his. When Resurrection Day approached, I witnessed an unexpected decline in respect for my beliefs. The relationship went awry. In my opinion, it did so solely based on our having been unequally yoked.

We had been celebrating our Easter/Resurrection Day all week. I was serving as Youth Pastor at a church, and we were dramatizing the passion play. My husband attended both the Good Friday and Resurrection Day services. On Easter Sunday, after worship, which was so sacred to me, and after I had cooked the most amazing Resurrection Day dinner (he had eaten his fill), my husband stated to me, "It did not happen."

His statement took me so far aback. I was on a spiritual high from celebrating the whole week and from leading worship and impacting the lives of many. I was also pumped about being with him, although he was of a different faith, and having had him come and support me. We were indeed the example. But when he turned and told me that the resurrection never happened, it was like a blow to the head. It was certainly a blow to my heart. It was baffling to me to know that after watching and listening, after seeing and hearing the scriptures dramatized, it was so easy for him to say that the resurrection did not happen.

It was at that moment then I realized how much of a Christian I was, and how strong a believer I was. It was at that moment when I thought I gained clarity of what it meant to really love the Lord. I was not going to be told that my story of Jesus was not real. I was not going to be told that the events in Christ's life did not happen, for to allow such an abominable statement or blasphemous statement is to decry my faith. For me, his negative declaration was the most insulting thing that could ever have been done to me. To have the person I love, the person I had agreed to marry as my soulmate, tell me blatantly that my beliefs were not real was hurtful and offensive beyond measure. It was insensitive because it was said on our holiest of days, one of the pinnacle days of our faith—the day when Christ is risen. It was not only offensive, but it was painful. To have the person I loved be so insensitive as to say that during my celebratory hour, made me question his love for me. How can he say that he loves me? I never would have done that to him. I questioned his love, and I knew at that moment what was meant by my Pastor when he spoke of being unequally yoked and declared that we should unite with someone of the same religious beliefs. I knew firsthand the impact of it, and I knew I would not survive it. I knew being in a relationship in which I was unequally yoke regarding my faith was not going to work. And it was at that moment that I began changing and realizing the relationship had to go. So, I went to God in prayer.

Prayer:

"Dear God: Your girl has messed up. Please forgive me. I tried to choose without prejudice, but I cannot believe that I have chosen a man in my life who does just enough to get by, leaving me to carry the load, and has the gall to be so callous as to decry Jesus on our holiest of days in the midst of eating the holiday meal that I had spent all day preparing. God, I just don't believe that you would want me with a man who would not even try to understand your story.

And God, I certainly do not believe that you want me taking care of a man. I know you did not bring me this far just to be with someone so disrespectful and who lacks such drive and determination so that I could fulfill his responsibilities as a man. I realize that we are unequally yoked, God, and I am so sad about it. It hurts a lot. I can't spend the rest of my life taking care of a man. Oh, Lord, help me! Help me! Help me!"

The tears would not stop falling. I was praying, but at this point in the prayer, I didn't even know for what to ask. I just knew that I was desperate. I knew that I wanted him gone so that I did not have to take care of him, but I did not know if I wanted him all the way gone, or faraway gone, or part-of-the-way gone; I just didn't know. I also knew that I did not want him hurt or dead, so, I just did not know what to pray for. So, I continued:

"God, please remove him from my life without causing him bodily harm. I don't know what this means, nor do I know what it looks like. It's your call, my Lord. In the name of Jesus, I pray. Amen."

I cried so much that night. The tears wouldn't stop. I knew it was a long shot. How would God get me out of this one? I didn't even know if God would even try. I did this. This was my doing. I married someone of a different faith, believing that somehow it could work. I got myself into it. My ex-husband's song had always been "I am not going back to Africa. You can't make me go back there. There is no way I am ever going back there. Sleeping on the floor in Chicago is better than sleeping in the bed in Africa." I didn't understand it, but I heard his passion, and I knew that there was no way he was going back. However, within two weeks of my prayer to God, the most astonishing thing happened.

God's Answer:

We were eating dinner when out of the blue, my husband blurted out, "Baby, I'm going." Now, I didn't know what he was talking about. I didn't know what he meant. So, I asked him, "Huh? What do you mean, you're going? Going where?"

"Home," he said. "I'm going back to Africa." I was stunned! I was in total disbelief, yet I said nothing. I wanted him to continue. He went on to tell me that it was time for him to go back home. My husband spoke of the two daughters he had left there ten years earlier and told me that they needed him. He said that he could work there and come back here. "Come back?" I thought to myself. There were some deportation issues at play, so, I warned him that if he went back to Africa, I would not fight for him to come back. I do not think he believed me.

I could not believe what I was hearing. The man who vowed never to go back there was now telling me that he was going. And I knew that this was God. So, I gathered up my money we went to his travel-agent friend, and we purchased his one-way ticket. He left days after attending doctoral graduation. I was able to divorce him with only $650, as I was enrolled in the legal aid benefit at my job. I only had to pay court costs for the services of my attorney. What a blessing! What a miracle! God had answered my prayer in a mighty way.

Lesson:

When we are in right relationship with God, God allows for our mistakes and God is gracious and forgiving and will not hold us to them. God loves us so much that he will even help us through the consequences of our mistakes, as God did with me. Do not think that just because you made a mistake, God's hand is removed from your life. It is not.

In this experience, I did not even know what to pray. In fact, I believed that I had messed up so badly that I didn't even think I had the right to pray to God about it. But the scripture says that God is faithful and just to forgive. So, I stepped out on faith and prayed my oh-so-selfish prayer anyway. Once we have accepted the Lord, Jesus into our lives and express our faith and become faithful believers and followers of Christ, our relationship with God begins. We can nurture ourselves in this relationship by praying and trusting God. Because of my relationship with God, I knew that God was there, and I knew that God was powerful. In addition, I knew that God loved me, and that God hears me. Whether God would answer me favorably, I did not know. But I knew that I could go to him and at least tell him of my troubles. You can, too. God will demonstrate God's faithfulness to us time and time again. God is a faithful God. God loves us in spite of us, despite our foolishness, despite our mistakes. God is faithful to me, and God is faithful to you. God will be faithful to us, as believers for the rest of our days. Hallelujah, hallelujah! Thank you, Lord! Amen!

Song:

He's Been Faithful (Vicki Yohe)

In my moment of fear
Through every pain, every tear
There is a God who is faithful to me
When my strength is all gone
And my heart has no song
There's a God who is faithful to me
Every word he has promised is true
What I thought was impossible I've seen my God do
He's been faithful, faithful to me

Desires of the Heart: From Doctoral Student to Seminary Teacher

Scripture:

"Ask, and it will be given to you; Seek, and you will find; Knock, and it will be opened to you." Matthew 7: 7 (ESV)

This relationship experience is twofold. It is regarding my desire to obtain a Doctor of Ministry degree and the amazing opportunity that occurred as a result. A friend of mine, whom I met while pursuing my Master of Divinity degree at the Chicago Theological Seminary, went on to pursue his Doctor of Ministry degree from the United Theological Seminary in Dayton, Ohio, a few years after our graduation. Near the end of his studies, he sent me an email that said he was about to graduate. He emailed me a picture of his degree being conferred upon him and stated that the journey was over and that he had done it. We had graduated only five years earlier, and now he was sending me emails with pictures of himself being enstooled as a Doctor of Ministry from one of the most prolific theological seminaries in the United States. I was proud of him, and I told him so. I admired his levels of intelligence and discipline. Although he was younger than I, I considered him ministry-education role model.

At that moment, after looking at his graduation picture, I was inspired. I felt in my spirit a desire to get a doctorate someday:

Unspoken Prayer/Heart's Desire:

"I wish I could get a doctorate someday."

That was all I said. And yes, the enemy started to fill my thoughts with seeds of doubt: "Oh, never mind. I'm not smart enough to get a Doctorate. I would not even qualify for any of their programs. There is no way I would be able to go down to the seminary to take classes." So, naturally, I dismissed the idea.

God's Answer:

The next thing I knew in a couple of weeks, my friend, Dr. Damon Jones sent me another email inviting me to join his Doctor of Ministry group with a focus on Christian Education. I could not believe it. I had only whispered the thought to myself. I had only whispered the desire of my heart to get a doctoral degree. And now here was the opportunity to do so right in front of me. Not only was it right in front of me, but the group was going to be led by my dear friend, a fact that alleviated much of my insecurity. This was indeed a blessing from God. I grew excited. I called him and asked him all kinds of questions and he answered them all. And within a month after applying, I was accepted. I was on my way to earning my Doctor of Ministry degree in a class led by a dear friend of mine. It meant that I had to do well. I did not want to embarrass myself. I wanted to represent God in Christ. I wanted to reflect intelligence. God had answered that desire of my heart.

Scripture:

"Delight thyself also in the LORD; and he shall give thee the desires of thine heart."

Psalms 37:4 ESV

Out of all my educational experiences, I must say that earning my Doctorate degree in ministry has proven to be the most rewarding. I found the process invigorating because it was through that journey that I discovered my ministry purpose and where my deepest interests lie. I learned how to conduct research and how to report that research after its analysis. The process was so fulfilling and rewarding to me that it enticed me for a moment to want to be the mentor of a group at the seminary. Yes, I wanted to be a seminary professor. I remember entertaining that notion and for a split second and simply just uttering the words:

Prayer:

"God, I'd like to be a mentor one day."

That' was all I said. I expected nothing. It was just a statement of a desire of my heart. I was surprised how that the enemy quickly reared its discouraging head by reminding me that I had no college-level teaching experience, and that to have a group meant that I had to recruit my own students, and that I did not know enough people who were at the doctoral level to even begin to think about recruiting my own people. Therefore, I dismissed the idea immediately. It was a mere passing thought.

God's Answer:

At the end of my class's defense, we were all headed over to celebrate our newly accomplished title of "Doctor of Ministry," by having dinner at a local restaurant. I remember asking my mentor and friend, Dr. Damon Jones, a question about mentorship just to quench my curiosity. "Dr. Jones, how much do mentors make," I asked. I found his response to be rather evasive: "We'll talk about that after dinner." I conceded and we got into our cars and went on to the restaurant. After dinner, he and I were walking out to our cars. I was expecting and interested to hear what he had to say about mentor pay, but what he said stunned me. "Well, Elaine, you asked me how much mentors make, and I want you to know that it is funny you should ask, because Dr. Neil (his co-mentor) and I believe that you would be the best person to take over the group." I was puzzled. So, I responded with a bewildered, "Huh?" Dr. Jones continued, "Dr. Neil and I have been discussing who would be the best person to take my place as his partner mentor because I am leaving, and we decided that you would be the best person to replace me." I was shocked. I could not believe what I was hearing. So, I delved further. "You know, if this is your idea of a joke, it's not very funny." Dr. Jones' reply was simply, "No, Elaine, it is not a joke. Would you consider being the mentor with Dr. Neil next year?" I was speechless for a moment. I knew I had only uttered my desire to be a mentor. I had only whispered my desire to God, and God has answered my utterance with that desire of my heart. We walked mover to Dr. Neil, and he concurred with what Dr. Jones was saying. I told them both that I needed to pray on it for a moment. I already knew I would accept the position. I did not know how it was going to work out because I was a full-time Assistant Principal. I just knew that it was something my heart desired. God had granted me the desire of my heart. For that, I praise him right now.

Lesson:

The lesson here is simple yet powerful. When I first entered the doctoral program, I made a vow to God that I would do my best. I wanted to make sure I gave God my all because I wanted to be successful. I was determined to confirm through my work ethic that I was indeed called. That was important to me. I cannot say that my confidence level was high because earning a doctorate degree was something unimaginable to me. I knew I wanted it. But being able to attain it was something of which I was not confident. I wanted God to get the glory through my studies I wanted nothing more than to reflect God throughout this journey. It was imperative. So, I promised God that I would do my best and asked God to do the rest. . That has always been my philosophy— "Do my best and let God do the rest." And that is what I did.

I made timelines to keep myself on schedule and shared them with my classmates. During the holidays I gave gifts to all of them because I appreciated being a part of the group. I enjoyed it so much. It is fair to say that I kept my eyes and my mind stayed on God the whole time I was in the program. I did so because I wanted to please God as a student. I wanted God to be proud of me as a student in ministry. I wanted to represent a quality student because that is what God deserves from my life. And because I kept my eyes and my mind on God, God granted me the desires of my heart—first, to obtain a Doctor of Ministry Degree, and second, to become a mentor/teacher of a group. Becoming a mentor was the best job I have ever had in my entire life, for it was fulfilling and revealed the truth of who I was. I praise God for that humbling, yet exulting opportunity! God is something else!

God repeatedly demonstrates in our lives that God is faithful to us. We must allow these demonstrations to nurture our relationship with God. Our faith should grow; our trust should grow; and our dependence upon God should grow. As we demonstrate our reverence for God through our faith, and our lives, God will continue to pour out God's grace and mercy upon us in the form of blessings, both tangible and intangible. We must put God first in our lives. We must seek to serve God in all that we do. More emphatically, we must do it eagerly, expecting nothing in return.

Give your all to God. Keep your mind on God, keep your eye on the prize, and there is nothing that God will not allow you not to have or achieve. Amen, glory to God!

Songs:

He's A Keepa (Norwegian Gospel Voices)

He'll keep you in perfect peace
Just keep your mind stayed on him
He'll keep you in perfect peace
If you keep your mind on him.

The Grace of God (GMWA Mass Choir)

Grace of God
Sweet grace of God
That taught me, brought me.
Grace of God, sweet grace of God,
That brought me, taught me

Already Worked It Out: Joiner and Joan

Scripture:

"But thou, O Lord, art a shield for me; my glory and the lifter up of mine head."

Psalm 3 (KJV)

It was July 18th, and, in a few days, I was going to be ordained. I couldn't believe it. I actually had made it through to this point. I had stood before the various councils and committees and had been approved for ordination. Boy, was I excited.! I had family members coming up to Chicago from South Carolina— my mom, sister, brothers, nieces, and nephews. I had friends coming from both South Carolina and Philadelphia. Plus, I had people who supported me in Chicago all coming to support me as an ordinand. I could not have been more humbled or excited.

One of my brothers and sister-in law were catering the food. They were fixing just the best dishes! I wanted to have so much tasty food for everyone to eat because they came out to support me. I had planned to have a nice spread in the room for the pastors who were going to process in in my honor. I wanted them to be comfortable with snacks and hors d'oeuvres and drinks. I simply cannot express the excitement I felt!

Because of scheduling conflicts at my home church, I decided to have my ordination at the church at which I served (Immanuel Bethel United Church of Christ). I had delegated the task of picking up my programs from my home church to a dear colleague, Rev. Ethel Southern, as Trinity had graciously assumed the responsibility of drafting, designing, and printing the programs. I had edited them earlier in the week and could not wait to see them. I just wanted them to be perfect. My decorating team and the caterers and I were all meeting at Immanuel Bethel at 10:00 Saturday morning. Rev. Ethel was bringing the programs., as well. When the programs arrived, I eagerly opened the box. What I found was astonishingly disappointing. My last name "Joyner," was misspelled. I could not believe it! Instead of spelling "Joyner" with a "y," as it has been spelled throughout all my official documents at the church through all my giving envelopes, membership dues payments, and resolutions, it was spelled with an "i." "What!" I exclaimed. "Why is there an "I "here? They know how to spell my name. How could they make such error? When I had edited it earlier it was not spelled that way." I was frantic. I tried to call the clerk at the church but received no answer. I had left messages at the church yet received no call back. I was indeed very frustrated! I did not have time to deal with the "why" of it all, however. That would have done no good for such a time as this. The important question was, "Now, what was I going to do?" Help me. Amen."

One of my best friends, Joan, had come to celebrate with me from Columbia, and was helping me decorate. Joan and I have been friends since the ninth grade. That's a long time. Joan saw that I was clearly upset and asked me what was wrong. I explained to her that I wouldn't have any programs at my ordination because my name was misspelled on the program.

Now, I am going to briefly discuss Joan's theory about what happened. She considered this occurrence one of sabotage, that it had been done on purpose. She questioned that If I had edited the programs earlier in the week, and that mistake was not there, then how and why was it there now? While I heard and understood what she was saying, I was excited about being both confirmed and affirmed by the Christian community. I was excited that my mom and family and friends have come out to support me. Therefore, I was not about to let the enemy destroy my joy by focusing on the negative. I have never been one to let anyone destroy my joy because my joy never came from anyone. My joy has always come from the Lord. I did not know how I was going to get through this problem, but I knew that God had not brought me this far to leave me. I also knew that it was God who was ordaining me, and since it was God who was ordaining me, God would get the glory through my ordination. I believe that the enemy knew that God would Get the glory from my ordination, as well, and the work that I was going to do in the Lord. I will say briefly, however, that although I was not even going to discuss the notion of sabotage, when I thought about it, Joan's theory of sabotage was probably accurate, and frankly, I knew of its origin (or at least one of the human vessels through which the enemy operated in this attempt). I won't give any names because I still refuse to elevate the enemy through my work. I was not going to allow my main concern at the time to be the enemy. My main concern was getting programs to pass out to all my guests. I was terribly upset. It was then that I offered my prayer to God.

Prayer:

"Lord, help me!"

I ranted and raved about those programs! My mom saw my anguish. My niece and nephews saw my anguish. My students at the church saw my anguish. Everyone saw my anguish and my disappointment. But no one could help. Then, my girlfriend, Joan, came to me.

God's Answer:

"Elaine, where are those programs," she asked. "They're over there, "I responded, as I pointed in their direction. She walked over, picked up one of the programs, examined the front, and began turning the pages. Then out of the blue, she offered a solution. "Elaine, I can fix this." "Huh," I replied. "You know I do calligraphy. I can fix this," she continued. I have to be honest and say that my first mental reaction was that I didn't want any jacked-up programs. I didn't want people talking about the tackiness of my programs. But Joan assured me or reminded me that her handwriting had always been artistic, and that she could write like anybody. She assured me that the correction would only be noticeable if one were looking for it. I thought to myself, "What other choice do I have? "Joan went on to tell me that all she needed was a black calligraphy pen. She and my sister-in-law went to the nearby arts and crafts store and brought back a few pens, and my girlfriend, Joan, the calligrapher, sat down and corrected 300 programs by hand, and made them look flawless. Instead of changing the "y" to "i," Joan changed the "i" to "y" and put some respect on my name. And my problem was solved.

Lesson:

Let the record show: when God has a plan, or when something is within God's plan, it shall come into fruition. It will be executed. There is nothing that will be able to stop it. And although Satan tries because Satan knows the incredulity of the heights to which God is going to be glorified through your work, Satan cannot stop what is within the will of God. It took me only a moment to recognize God's hand in this crisis. You see, I had to talk Joan into coming to my ordination. She didn't like long trips and she never liked flying. That was why she had never come to Chicago to visit me before. I told her how important it was for my best friend to be at my ordination and that I would have been extremely disappointed had she not come. So, as a friend would do, she came both to help out and to attend my ordination. Just that fact alone let me know that while I was trying to figure it out, God had already worked it out. While I had no idea this situation would arise, our God, who knows all and sees all, was fully aware, and had already made preparations for its resolve. That's love, y'all. And it is humbling beyond measure. This is nine years later, and I still shed tears about God's love for me. I still shed tears about how God has shown God's faithfulness to me in this and all situations. God's omnipresence is real. God's omniscience is real. Do not ever discount them. God's love is real. Even when we don't know what we need, God has already supplied our need. When you face your trials and tribulations and have been in an active relationship with God, you can rest assured that whatever the problem is, God has already worked it out. Thank you, Lord, Lord! Thank you for your love! Thank you for friends! Thank you for Joan! Hallelujah to Jesus! I praised God then, and I praise God now.

Song:

Jesus Can Work It Out (Charles G. Hayes)

That problem that I had
I just couldn't seem to solve
I tried and I tried
But I kept gettin' deeper involved
So, I turned it over to Jesus
And I stopped worryin' about it
Turned it over to the Lord
(He worked it out)

Song:

Thou Art A Shield for Me: Psalm 3 (Byron Cage)

Lord, how are they increased that trouble me,
Many are they that rise up against me.
Many there be which say of my soul,
There is no help for Him in God.

But Thou, O Lord, art a shield for me;
My glory, You lift mine head.
But Thou, O Lord, art a shield for me;
My glory, the lifter up of mine head.

Fortifying A Flattened Faith

Scripture:

"And when he got into the boat, his disciples followed him. And behold, there arose a great storm on the sea, so that the boat was being swamped by the waves; but he was asleep. And they went and woke him, saying, "Save us, Lord; we are perishing." And he said to them, "Why are you afraid, O you of little faith?" Then he rose and rebuked the winds and the sea, and there was a great calm. And the men marveled, saying, "What sort of man is this, that even winds and sea obey him?"

Matthew 8: 23-27 (ESV)

There was a woman, who, no matter what kind of car she drove, repeatedly found herself getting a flat tire. Whether it was her first set of wheels, which was fifteen years old at purchase, or one of her brand-new "smart cars" of today, which she purchased every two or three years, she always seemed to wind up with a flat tire. It didn't even matter where she was going or from where she was coming, or even that she put Michelins on every car she drove, she still wound up with a FLAT TIRE! She took a trip out of town, upon her arrival at her hotel she found herself with a flat tire. She drove to the university in pursuit of her Master's Degree; and upon her arrival, she found that she had a flat tire. On her way to work one morning, about three blocks away from her home, she found that she had a flat tire. The woman worked nights so safety was an issue to her and the thought of getting a flat tire caused her much anxiety and fear—fear about whether or not she was going to have the money to pay for this unplanned emergency, and fear about whether some stranger would come by and do her harm, as she had often heard reported on the local news.

One night, at about 2:00 a.m., while on her way home from work, the woman encountered a major traffic jam. Cars were backed up for blocks. And although she did not know the cause, the woman could tell that whatever it was that was happening, was a **BIG DEAL,** for the streets had been lit extra-bright by generator-powered lamps and police cars were lined up along each block of side streets that she had passed. The woman rolled down her window a bit to hear the conversations of the other motorists, and learned that a bicycle race, the Tour de France, was coming through, and their plotted route had caused traffic back-ups in several areas of the city. Police officers were directing traffic up ahead, allowing for the passage of cars only when there were no cyclists in sight.

As she sat in her car awaiting her turn to pass through the blocked intersection, she heard a car horn. She looked over and saw a male motorist trying to get her attention. Now, of course, this made the woman quite nervous, for she was out by herself, at 2:00 in the morning, in a situation from which she could not move. So she did what

every intelligent, safety-conscious woman would do—
IGNORED HIM!

"He may as well stop blowing his horn at me, cause it's 2:00 in the morning, I'm out here by myself, and I'm not trying to have any conversation with a strange man." But the man was persistent! He kept blowing at her, until finally she acknowledged his efforts. She looked over at him quickly and suspiciously; and much to her surprise, he was not trying to make conversation. Instead, he was making a pointing gesture at her front tire. "You have a flat tire," the man said. Your tire, it's flat! And he did not offer to help her, either. I guess since the woman had ignored him so badly, he just left her on her own. He knew that woman needed help. Immediately, for the woman, that all-too-familiar panic set in. **She had another flat tire!**

What was she going to do? There she was out alone, in the middle of the night, with a flat tire! Should she get out of the car and call herself fixing it? She was stuck in traffic that was moving at the pace of a baby's crawl and thought about the understandable anger of the other motorists if she clogged up an already frustrating traffic jam. So she opted not to get out, but to do what she had done every other time she'd gotten a flat tire— Cry! As she cried, she remembered that she'd just purchased a cell phone; so she searched frantically for the phone and called her husband.

"I have a flat," she said. I am sitting in traffic, and I have a flat. This man told me. I didn't even know it." The more she talked the more she cried. Her husband, in his efforts to calm her assured her that he was on his way. Through her tears she explained to her husband that her old apartment building was across the intersection and that she would be allowed to pass through the intersection soon, and that was where she would wait for him. The woman did not want to hang up the phone, but her battery power was low, and she might need it in case of her husband could not locate her. So, with reluctance, she hung up. And oh, did her tears start to flow! They flowed like a faucet with a worn-out washer ring. She cried and shivered and cried and sweated and cried, and cried, and cried…. She was consumed by her fear and anxiety and began to think of the most dangerous possibilities that lurked in her media-affected imagination. What if…someone posed as a helper, but instead proved to be a perpetrator of a violent crime against her? You know, instead and kidnapped at gunpoint her and caused her bodily harm? What if…someone came and robbed her, beaten her, or even tried to kill her? At the height of her fear and anxiety, the woman cried out, **"God, why do you keep letting this happen to me? You know I'm scared! You know I'm working! I'm not just hanging out. I'm working! I do my part! I buy the best tires! I buy a new car every two to three years so I can be safe; and you just still just keep on letting this happen to me!**

I submit to you that not only had the air gone out of the woman's tires, but at this moment, because she'd had repeated flat-tire experiences, and because this flat-tire incident seemed to be the most frightening one of all, it is fair to say that the woman's faith had deflated, as well. The air in her raft of faith, which had kept her afloat throughout all her difficult trials in the past, seemed to have been let out in this final flat-tire incident. And thus, at that moment, she had a flat faith.

As we look at our Scriptures, we find a comparable situation in which the disciples find themselves out on a boat, in a ferocious windstorm. This windstorm is so fierce that it brings flooding waters into the boat, so much that the disciples think they are going to drown or perish. Have you ever been in a storm that seemed so ferocious that you thought you would be swallowed up or destroyed by it, causing your faith to flatten?

It doesn't have to be a windstorm of nature such as that which the disciples experienced, but one of the windstorms of life? Like an employment windstorm, in which there's discrimination on the job? Every six months, at wage review time, there is always some reason you qualify for only one-third of the percentage increase of your European counterparts. Or even worse, you are denied a promotion because it was given instead to someone younger than you, with less education than you, less experience than you, and who was even trained by you, but because they are of European descent (white), they got the promotion over you that was long overdue you. You do your best! You study hard, you get to work early, and leave late; and you give your 200%, which is a mandate just because you're African American, but none of it matters; cause each time you are passed over and disappointed by yet another excuse as to why you did not qualify. And slowly, the air in your raft of faith is seeping out and you find yourself with a flat faith.

Or a financial windstorm—you have followed the recipe for fulfilling the "American Dream," taken your savings and invested in stocks because you've witnessed the market on Wall Street make record climbs in record times. **Do you remember a few years back when it seemed like every**

day on the news the market on Wall Street rose by 100 points or more? I mean, the news reporters were smiling, CEOs were being highlighted as "super-CEOs" when their company's stocks did well, and everybody was just ecstatic? I mean, people who never even thought about the stock market, saw all that excitement and were walking around talking about the STOCK MARKET, and ONLINE TRADING, trading one and two shares, talking about they were goanna be rich! Just had to get in on some of that action! So, you studied the numbers, took your life's savings, and only invested in the top ten companies. And in less than a year, you witnessed the robbery of a lifetime, **(well, except for the one committed by your President as he robbed this country of its democratic process in the presidential election, and the oil control robbery he's in the process of committing now, using your family members and mine),** but in less than a year, the Houston-based Enron Corporation, the 7th largest company in America, with over 20,000 employees (about the seating capacity of Madison Square Garden), a reported net income of $979 million in the year 2000 alone, and stocks that at their highest point, were valued at $90 per share was revealed in a scandal that would rock the nation. A company whose numbers you believed would take you over the top, and have you set for the rest of your life, announced that its Chief Executive Officer, Kenneth Lay, and six other board of directors on its audit committee, had withheld debt information, and falsified earnings records; and while he was fully aware of the company's financial woes, CEO Lay, underhandedly sold his Enron stock, but misled employees as to the true values of the stocks in order to keep them from accessing their retirement accounts and selling theirs. And as a result, by the end of 2001, stocks that were valued at $90 per share at the beginning of the year, was devalued to a meager sixty-seven cents by year's end. Enron folded; your life's savings fizzled; and your faith was flattened.

Or maybe it's an abusive windstorm. No matter what you do to please your spouse, it's never enough! The house is not clean enough; the food isn't hot enough; the kids are making too much noise; you were on the phone too long; the bed is not fresh enough; your hair is a mess; you do not have any make-up on; you've got TOO MUCH make-up on; that dress is too short; this dress is too long! And for that, you deserve a smack, and another, and another—You are afraid to tell it, cause you're afraid of what he will do to you then. God, where are you? Flattening your faith…

Maybe it was a **PROVIDER** windstorm. You are making six figures (or close to it), but you're the only one in the family who is employed. Your wife is a stay-at-home Mom, for you have five kids, two of whom are in college, and the other three you will not entrust to a daycare center. Your family wants to wear the best, and ride in the best, and live in the best of neighborhoods. Got to have some Airforce Ones. Need a new St. Johns suit for the Women's Day program. That little Hummer is affordable, isn't it? You are struggling to make ends meet, but they don't understand. All they know is that Daddy's making **"six figures."** My daddy makes a lot of money. Little do they realize that those six figures divided by seven mouths, and compounded by five-figure tuition costs, four-figure annual vacation costs, a mortgage, a car note, and utilities, leave little more than a two-pound headache from the therapy bill you accumulate as you try to **FIGURE** out how to get out of debt! You can't explain your troubles to your family, for fear of being deemed "less than a man." The creditors are calling, and the stress is overwhelming. And slowly, there goes your faith—flattened!

I can go on and on naming life's windstorms, but time won't allow it. I could talk about health windstorms, in which you go to the doctor for a regular check-up and find yourself with an unexpected diagnosis, one that seems to have come out of nowhere and alters your presupposed lengthy life span.

Or even a breach-of-trust windstorm, in which you find out that your spouse has been unfaithful, and it's pulling at your insides. You love your spouse, but right now you hate your spouse; you trusted, but NEVER again; you made sacrifices, and for what? You believed in the institution of marriage. Your marriage was ordained by God. How could this happen? Pssssssss— flattened!

And married people are not the only ones who encounter windstorms. Single people do, too. Singles, you know, that all-too-familiar need or yours— "I just want to find that somebody special —somebody to love, somebody to love me; somebody to laugh with, cry with, dream with, share new experiences with; **somebody to keep me warm during those cold winter nights.** I'm intelligent, good-looking, have a good job, good salary, just got it going on. But God, why won't you send me my soulmate? Pssss… flat! **Oh, those dreadful windstorms of life….**

Let's look at our text. Verse 23 says, "And when he got into the boat, the disciples followed him." This verse is especially important because it tells us that the disciples were followers of Jesus. They followed Jesus, and yet they were about to encounter a windstorm so powerful that they feared they would be totally consumed or destroyed by it. There is a particularly important message here of which we need to take care to note. This text tells us that **EVEN** followers of Christ encounter harsh windstorms. Look over and tell your neighbor, **"Neighbor, I know you're a follower of Christ, but even YOU are not exempt from life's windstorms."** Now look over at your other neighbor and say, **"And neither are you!"** That's right! Even followers of Christ find themselves facing harsh windstorms.

And when this windstorm arose, verse 25 says that they went and awoke Jesus, and demanded his immediate attention. **"Lord, save us! We are perishing!"** Now isn't that typical of us when we find ourselves in our storms? We want God to stop what God is doing and to come see about us on the double! Even those storms we bring upon ourselves. And have the gall to call God and demand God to get us out. Oh, you don't demand when you bring it on yourself? Oh, by that time, you're begging? Oh. These disciples were no different. Jesus was asleep. Up came a windstorm, and the disciples woke Jesus up out of his sleep to save them from perishing.

Jesus' response is quite an attention-getter. He did not go into a panic, as had his disciples and as do we. He felt the boat shaking as it was being tossed by the turbulence of the waves. And I'm sure he could see the water as it filled the boat! But Jesus' initial response did not even address the storm at all. Instead, what he addressed the disciples' state of distress. Jesus questioned, **"Why are you afraid,"** for he didn't understand it. Then he labeled the disciples according to his observations of them and their handling of themselves in the storm. **"You of little faith?"** Be careful how you handle yourself in your windstorm, because according to this text, the way you handle yourself is indicative of your level of faith! Jesus sensed through the disciples' panic that their level of faith was quite small or even **flat**, like the woman in our story. Scholars say their faith was weak and Jesus rebuked it. Jesus rebukes weak, flat faith! What did Jesus observe? I submit to you that Jesus observed four indications of a flat faith —1) fear, 2) fret, 3) forget, and 3) forfeit. The disciples displayed these indications, the woman in our story displayed them, and so do most of us when we find ourselves in our storms.

When our faith has been flattened, the first thing we do is

—FEAR the worst and fabricate feelings of forlornness, or distress. The disciples immediately thought of the worst thing that could happen as they cried, "We are perishing!" And so did the woman in our story, as she thought about getting robbed, beaten, or killed. What do you think about in your financial storm? That you're going to be evicted from your home? Kicked out the club? You're going to feel ashamed? What are your immediate thoughts?

The next thing we do when our faith is flat is

—FRET about the failure as if it were the force that navigate our existence.

The disciples fretted about that boat sinking as if the boat were the force that kept them alive and safe. The boat was just the object, but the force and the source, was the man asleep in another part of the boat. God is the source that navigates our existence! The woman with the flat tire fretted through her tears about her flat tire, as if it were those tires that were the source of her safety. The tires were mere objects. God is the source of her safe existence! What about when you or someone you love gets that unexpected diagnosis? Do you fret about a life span that has been "cut short"? It is not this life that you ought to be concerned about. It is eternal life for which you ought to yearn.

The third thing we do when we have a flat faith is

—Forfeit God's blessings by focusing on the failed aspects of the situation. Oftentimes we miss the blessings of God by focusing on the negatives of the situation. The disciples, so caught up in the notion of a sinking boat, failed to realize the significance of the presence of Jesus. Now I am not talking about the whether they realized that Jesus was there. Of course, they knew that. But what this text indicates is that they did not recognize what the fact that Jesus' presence with them meant. You know, sometimes, we who call ourselves "followers of Christ," in our humanness, fail to realize what that means, especially when we find ourselves facing a crisis. Jesus was right there in the boat with them. They followed him into the boat. Did they think that Jesus was going to let the boat sink and that Jesus was going to just drown? I mean, knowing that Jesus was present should have been enough!! You would think they would have thought something like, I mean knowing Jesus was sleeping back in the other room, "Shoot, Jesus back there, ain't nothing gon' happen to this boat!" But that's just me. The disciples were so caught up in the water filling the boat and the intensity of the storm, that they could not even see the real blessing, as it was right before them. Our woman also failed to realize God's blessings in the midst of her storm. You see, earlier I told you that no matter what kind of car she'd driven, or where she was going, the woman repeatedly got a flat tire. When you focus on the aspects of repeated flat tires and the dangers she faced, it does seem pretty gloomy. However, when we give it a little thought, instead of feeling sorry for her, we would rejoice with her, because the fact that she'd had so many flat tire incidences without any harm or danger ever having come near her is enough to shout about. **YES**, she took a trip out of town, but she didn't notice the flat until she was at her hotel; and **YES**, she got a flat when driving to school, but she didn't notice the flat until she'd arrived at school; and **YES**, she'd even had a flat on her way to work, but she noticed it three blocks from her home, right across from a Goodyear Tire Shop, where she pulled in, had it repaired, and made it to work on time! Ofttimes, we forfeit our own blessings by focusing on the negative!

And the last thing we do when we have a flat faith is

—FORGET that the current windstorm is only a foreshadow of God's faithfulness. You see, we forget that storms don't last forever, and because they don't last forever, God will bring us through our storm. We forget that God is forever faithful to us, and that this windstorm is merely another opportunity for God to prove God's faithfulness to us.

1. we **fear** the worst
2. we **fret** about the failure
3. we **forfeit** God's blessings
4. and we **forget** that the windstorm is just a foreshadow of God's faithfulness.

But I came with a message tonight. I know we are tossed daily in our windstorms of life, sometimes even to the point of succumbing. But instead of having fear, God wants you to have faith. Faith, when you can't see your way. Faith, when you have done all that you can do. Faith, when the doctors have done all they can do. Faith, when you have studied as hard as you can. Faith, when you have paid as much as you can. God wants us to have faith!

Instead of fretting from worry, God wants you to have freedom from worry by keeping your mind on God, even in the midst of your storm. Scholars say that we get God's blessing of righteousness (right relationship with God) when you have faith (that is, when we put our total trust in God, abandoning all reliance on our own efforts and putting full confidence in God, God's work, and God's promises.) Once we have the gift of righteousness, the assurance in Psalm 37:25 is ours, as it states, "I have been young and now am old, yet I have not seen the righteous forsaken or their children begging bread! When you're in right relationship with God, you will **not** be forsaken.

Instead of forfeiting God's blessings as if God were absent during our windstorm, God wants us to flourish as a result of God's blessings, as we take time during our storm to pinpoint God's presence and recognize it as a blessing. Then we must take the time, in the mist of our storm, to thank God for both, God's presence and blessings!

And instead of forgetting that our windstorm is only a foreshadow to God's faithfulness, God wants us to be familiar with facts of God's goodness. You see, sometimes our faith can be flattened by doubt or peril. Scholars in the *Zondervan Dictionary of Bible Themes assert* that faith is supposed to grow, and that a weak faith does not grow. Therefore, a flat faith, which is likened unto a weak faith, is one that does not grow as well. We know that in order for something to grow, it must have some sort of fortifying agents, sunlight air and water, for plants, and air for a tire. Zondervan suggests that knowledge of God's faithfulness causes our faith to grow. And I suggest that we have flashbacks of God's faithfulness to fortify our flattened faith. These flashbacks can be of God's faithfulness to either others or us, in antiquity or in our own lifetime. Let me make a few suggestions.

In a health windstorm? Flashback—Jesus healed a leper, a paralytic, a woman with an issue of blood, and I know God has even cured your cold once or twice.

Feeling alone? Flashback—John 14:8 I will not leave you comfortless: I will come to you.

In need of deliverance from either a toxic relationship or a toxic chemical dependence? Flashback—Mark 16:17 says, "And these signs shall accompany those who believe: by using my name they will cast out demons; they will speak in new tongues."

Experiencing Fear? Flashback— Isaiah 41:10—Fear not: for I am with thee: be not dismayed: for I am God: I will strengthen thee; yea, I will uphold thee with the right hand of my righteousness.

In a windstorm of grief? Flashback—O death, where is thy sting? O grave, where is thy victory? Blessed are they that mourn: for they shall be comforted. And God shall wipe away all tears from their eyes; and there shall be no more death, neither sorrow, nor crying, neither shall there be any more pain: for the former things are passed away.

And if you need evidence of God's presence in the storm of someone's life today, well take a look at yourself. You've experienced a Flattened Faith a time or two in your life, wouldn't you say? Come on. Think about it for a moment. We all have! Simon Peter did it in the Bible when Jesus commanded him to walk on the water! So I know we have done it in one way or another. We have yelled at God, doubted God, ignored God, shaken our fists at God, and questioned God! And what did God do to us in return?? Did God leave us in our storm to fend for ourselves? Did God's raft of faithfulness towards us deflate and allow us to succumb to our storm? No! Even after we dissed God with our arrogant selfishness, God remained faithful to us! Let's look one last time at the woman's story.

You see, I didn't tell you the rest of the story. I stopped at the woman's tears. But what happened next was something incredibly revelatory! The woman had cried so intensely that she had mad moved to that quiet stage. You know, that stage at which you are just tired of crying. Well, the woman had reached this stage and thus, sat quietly as she waited for her husband to arrive. But before he arrived, the **HOLY SPIRIT** paid her a visit and guided her through flashbacks of God's faithfulness to her. The Holy Spirit revealed to the woman that she was being unfair to God and had yelled at God unjustly. "Think, for a moment," it continued. The woman sat still and upright and listened quietly and attentively.

God has done nothing but cared for you in every flat-tire incident you've had. You know all those worst-case scenarios you've concocted in your mind? They really could have happened to you, but in all God's gracefulness, God said "no." You know all those times you realized your flats after you had arrived at your destinations? They could have happened while you were en route to your destinations and left you stranded by the side of the road, but in God's gracefulness, God said "no." The woman began to dry her tears. The Holy Spirit kept talking. "And look at you now. Look behind you. Yes, it's 2:00 in the morning, but the streets are lit up like day. Yes, you are by yourself, but look at all those police officers who are less than fifty feet away. And yes, you are fifteen miles away from home, but look at where you are. You are right in front of the building in which you used to live! You could not be safer! And do you know who's behind all this comfort in your storm? That's right. It was I, God. I love you! Don't you know that by now? I have shown you over and over again. How many times must I prove it to you?

When you find yourself in one of life's turbulent windstorms, I urge and you feel that you're about to be consumed, I urge you to look back at some of the storms you've faced in the past and figure out where God was in that storm. When you recognize God's presence in every one of your past storms, no matter how bad they may have been, you will also recognize that never again, when you face a storm, will you have to fear, fret, forfeit, or forget;

for you will know that God is present and already has your storm under control." And just as Jesus rebuked the winds, in our text, for the disciples of little faith, and the Holy Spirit rebuked the fear, fret, and forgetfulness in the woman's storm and fortified her flattened faith, God will rebuke the threatening elements in your storm and fortify your flattened faith. God bless you!

Song:

So You Would Know (Brooklyn Tabernacle Choir)

Didn't I wake you up this morning
Were you clothed in your right mind
When you walked on this problem
Didn't I step right in on time
When you got weak along life's journey
My angel carried you
So you would know just how much I love you

The Importance of Prayer

Scripture:

"Rejoice in the Lord always, and again I will say, rejoice. Let your reasonableness be known to everyone. The Lord is at hand, do not be anxious about anything, but in everything by prayer and supplication with thanksgiving let your requests be made known to God. And the peace of God, which surpasses all understanding, will guard your hearts and minds in Christ Jesus."
Philippians 4:4–7(ESV)

We are living in a day when we can, without hesitation, say that there is so much to worry about, or that there is so much for us to be anxious about. We have been existing in a COVID-19 pandemic for almost two full years now and the moment we think that we have made it through, and are on the other side, another variant rears its ugly face. There was the Delta variant, the Lambda variant, and now the Omicron variant, which has poised itself to be the most contagious variant of all. We have our politicians and others battling about mandating masks. We are taking risks riding on airplanes and going to dinner and social events, but the moment somebody sneezes, coughs, or sniffles, our antennae rise, and we begin looking at them out of our side eye to assess whether this is a situation from which we need to exit quickly or ask them to leave. We ask that person who is coughing or sneezing if they are all right, not because we care about them, but because we are worried that they might have COVID and that we might in turn get it, too. We are anxious about catching Covid-19.

We feel that we are within our rights to be anxious about inflation. Yes, inflation— today! Gas prices average $4.40 today, compared to its average of $2.21 a year ago and it has many of us on edge. Grocery prices are on the rise. Milk, eggs, cheese, canned goods— all are at inflated rates. Many of us are having to make choices and for goal many of the comforts in luxuries of the past so that we can afford the basic necessities of life and it is making us anxious. I heard a woman on the news declare that she can no longer get that Starbucks coffee every morning like she used to because she needs to be able to pay for gas to get to work. Another stated that she would have to get rid of her pet because she could no longer afford to feed it. Because of inflation many of us are being forced to make exceedingly tough decisions that result in our making huge sacrifices things we enjoy or love dearly. And it is making us anxious. How much longer, Lord? How much higher will these prices rise? Am I going to be able to afford my home in the future? We are anxious!

Need I mention the violence? We have violence in society to be anxious about today. Every day-shootings! Every day-- robberies! Every day—carjackings! Every day— murders! Every day—suicides! Every day—gang retaliation! Every day— mass shootings at schools! Every day—hate crimes, and now, hate crimes claiming self-defense! Every day—expressway shootings! Every day— children killing parents because they won't give them what they want or because parents tell them that it is time they go and fend for themselves as adults. Every day—airplane violence against staff. Every day—violence! Every day—violence! Every day—violence! We… Are… Anxious… About… The violence!

We African Americans have gotten so anxious that we are making a mass exodus from Chicago to get away from this mess. We want better for our children. We want better for ourselves! We cannot live like this! We will not live like this! Reverend Anthony Williams of the "I Want to Live" movement, has succeeded in getting the governor of Illinois, J. B. Pritzker, to declare violence a public health crisis. The president has done the same and allocated funds to address the issue. We are anxious about violence! Driving on the highway – we are anxious! Going from our cars to the grocery store – we are anxious! Leaving the bank – we are anxious! Shopping downtown or in malls in communities where we never thought we would have to be afraid – we are anxious! Is this going to be the day when I get attacked, robbed, or car jacked? Will my child make it back home from school today? Will I make it home today to see my family again? Anxious! Yes, there is so much to eat be anxious about in these perilous times in which we live.

And lastly, some of us are anxious merely about the holidays: our loved ones have passed on and this is our first holiday without them or our second, or our third. We miss them dearly and we wish we could share in the holidays with them. Or we don't have anyone to spend the holidays with.

We have gotten a divorce and no longer have our spouses. Or we have never had a spouse and we just don't want to endure this holiday season feeling lonely yet again; with no one to whom to say, "Merry Christmas!" or to say it to us! No one to whom to show our love with a gift or to return the same. And it's hard! And it hurts! And we feel anxious!

But on this third Sunday of Advent, when the theme is "joy, "I come to tell you today that even though the world presents challenges in our lives that might tend to bring us down, and make us anxious, there is a way to ease our anxiety. There is a way to rid ourselves of our anxiety altogether and rise from our anxiety to "Amen." Our scripture begins by telling us to "rejoice in the Lord always." Paul, in his letter to the church at Philippi tells the Philippians to rejoice. According to the Collins English dictionary, rejoice is defined as, "to feel joyful, to be delighted, to express great joy or happiness." Paul's directives are clear in themselves. They speak for themselves. But in our human frailty and societal suffering, we cannot help but to ask, "How can we be expected to rejoice when there's so much going wrong in our society and so much going wrong in our lives?" But church, we know that the word will not leave us hanging. God will not leave us hanging. So, let us look on further.

According to workingpreacher.com this passage of scripture illustrates Paul's awareness that although the Philippians have done well on their faith journey, many of them are having second thoughts about their faith, like us in our anxiety. Our anxiety is a second thought. Our doubts are second thoughts. But this pericope reveals to me that the way to deal with our second thoughts, our doubts, and our fears, and our anxiety is to develop a strong relationship with God that will give us confidence, security, and assurance, no matter the situation in which we find ourselves. In fact, this relationship should be the primary resource in addressing every situation, good and bad. I would like to suggest to you that the path to developing and solidifying this relationship with God is centered around prayer. In fact, it could be accomplished by asserting the acronym, "PAT,"— which stands for, "Pray, Ask, and Thank."

The first thing that we must do when dealing with anxiety and developing our relationship with God is to PRAY. We need to develop a posture of prayer. Prayer should be our first resort when we find ourselves feeling worried or anxious. Prayer should be our first resort when we find ourselves facing tough decisions. Prayer should be our first resort when we find ourselves celebrating the blessedness of God. You know the old saying— "If you're going to pray then don't worry. If you're going to worry, then don't pray." We have to let prayer replace our worry; let prayer replace our anxiety. Philippians 4:6 says, "Do not be anxious about anything, but in everything by prayer..." Everything by prayer! "Pray – that is the first step in dealing with anxiety and other situations and developing your relationship with God.

The second step in developing and solidifying your relationship with God, and thus, arising from anxiety to "Amen" is "A" – ask. "But in everything by prayer and supplication. "To supplicate means to ask humbly. We have to develop a posture of prayer and do it. Not just say that we are going to pray but pray for real. You know how we always say I'm going to pray for you and never do it? We must develop posture of prayer. Prayer should be a part system. Prayer should be a part of our strategy in dealing with life's situations. And when we pray, we must ask God for what it is that we want; for what we need. Everything by prayer and supplication – supplicate – ask! Tell God what's on your heart, humbly. Do not go to God like you're perfect. Go humbly before God and ask God what it is of which you are in need. You have heard the adage "You have not because you ask not." Do not be afraid to ask God for what you want. Asking is an integral part of prayer. It is in the answering where God reveals Godself more clearly to you – that God is listening, that God hears you, and that God will answer your prayer according to what God deems is best. Psalm 37:25 states, "I have been young and now I am old, yet I have not seen the righteous forsaken or his children begging for bread." When you are in right relationship with God, God will never forsake you. But you will not see this phenomenon if you don't ask. If you do not step out and trust God, try God, and ask God for whatever it is that your heart desires. This is especially important, Saints. It is important to developing and solidifying your relationship with God.

In the third step in arising from anxious to "Amen" and developing and solidifying our relationship with God is to "T"– thank God. "But with thanksgiving let your requests be made known to God." "With Thanksgiving" means thanking God. Acknowledge what God has done. Thank God for what God is doing right now and thank God for what God is going to do in the future. Give God thanks in all things. Even when things are not going as well as you would like, you can find the positive in the situation, for which you ought to give God thanks. Give God thanks in all things as you make your requests to God! PAT- pray, ask, thank! Pray, Ask, Thank! That is how you make it to "Amen!" That is how you develop your relationship with God! That is how God reveals Godself to you! You see, Saints, when we get to "Amen," when we get to our celebratory point, which is our "Amen" point, we are back at the beginning of today's scriptural passage. Rejoice in the Lord always. When we get to amen, the amen of our prayer, we can rest assured that God hears our humble cries. We can rest assured that our prayers have been and will be answered as they have been in the past. We can rest assured that God will not forsake us. That God will take care of us, as God has done throughout our lives. And when we give God thanks, it will take us to "Amen," because it is in our Thanksgiving that we recognize the goodness of God, the grace of God, the mercy of God, the fullness of God, the faithfulness of God, all in our lives alone!!!! We won't even have to look at what God has done for the rest of the world. We only need to examine our own lives. God has been extremely good! God has been extremely kind to us! Merciful and gracious to each and every one of us. The scripture says that God is at hand. That means that God is nearby. You can rest assured God is nearby. That is something to hold onto. So, PAT— Pray, Ask, and Thank God! Arise from anxiety to "Amen"! Develop your relationship with Christ! Solidify it. And the scripture assures you that the peace of God will guard your hearts and minds in Christ Jesus! Now that ought to shout you! When you PAT— PRAY, ASK, and THANK God; you will have peace that passes all understanding. Nobody will understand your happiness. Nobody will understand your joy in these perilous times. People will question why you are so happy when things are so disastrous all around you! Nobody will understand why you are so happy-go-lucky all the time. You will have joy, I tell ya! You will rejoice! In this season of Advent on this third Sunday when the theme is joy, DEVELOP YOUR RELATIONSHIP WITH GOD THROUGH PRAYER, AND ARISE FROM ANXIETY TO AMEN!

Printed in the United States
by Baker & Taylor Publisher Services